Area-Efficient VLSI Computation

ACM Doctoral Dissertation Award

1982 *Area-Efficient VLSI Computation*, Charles Eric Leiserson

Area-Efficient VLSI Computation

Charles Eric Leiserson

The MIT Press
Cambridge, Massachusetts
London, England

Publisher's note: This format is intended to reduce the cost of publishing certain works in book form and to shorten the gap between editorial preparation and final publication. Detailed editing and composition have been avoided by photographing the text of this book directly from the author's typescript or word-processor output.

The dissertation was submitted in October 1981 to the Department of Computer Science, Carnegie-Mellon University in partial fulfillment of the requirements for the degree of Doctor of Philosophy. The thesis research was sponsored in part by the Defense Advanced Research Projects Agency (DOD) ARPA Order No. 3597 which is monitored by the Air Force Avionics Laboratory Under Contract F33615-78-C-1551, by the National Science Foundation under Grant MCS 78-236-76, and by the Office of Naval Research under Contract N00014-76-C-0370. The views and conclusions contained in this document are those of the author and should not be interpreted as representing the official policies, either expressed or implied, of the Defense Advanced Research Projects Agency or the United States Government. Charles E. Leiserson was also supported by a Fannie and John Hertz Foundation fellowship.

Library of Congress Cataloging in Publication Data

Leiserson, Charles Eric.
   Area-efficient VLSI computation.

   (ACM-MIT Press doctoral dissertation award series ; 1)
   Bibliography: p.
   Includes index.
   1. Electronic digital computers--Circuits. 2. Integrated circuits--Very large scale integration.
I. Title. II. Title: Area-efficient V.L.S.I. computation.
III. Series.
TK7888.4.L44 1983   621.3819'5835   82-23954
ISBN 0-262-12102-6

Series Foreword

In 1981, the MIT Press made a suggestion to the Association for Computing Machinery (ACM). The idea was to initiate a competition that would determine the best doctoral dissertation each year in computer science and its related fields and to have the winner published by the MIT Press. In addition to the recognition thus provided, the long-term effect might well be greater attention to producing high-quality dissertations.

Based upon recommendations by the relevant ACM organizational units, the ACM Council subsequently adopted the suggestion. A doctoral dissertation award program was established. The award consists of one thousand dollars provided by ACM to the author of the winning dissertation and royalties paid to the author by the MIT Press. A process was set up by ACM to use technically knowledgeable volunteers to screen the submissions and to make the final selection. Universities and colleges granting Ph.D.'s in computer-related sciences were invited to make submissions. Each university or college is limited to submitting only the one best dissertation accepted by the institution between July 1st and the following June 30th for each academic year.

The award is to be presented annually at ACM's Computer Science Conference.

The program began in early 1982. This volume is the first winner to be published in this new program.

The winner of the 1982 ACM doctoral dissertation award is *Area-Efficient VLSI Computation*, written by Charles Eric Leiserson while at Carnegie-Mellon University. The thesis work was supervised by Professors Jon L. Bentley and H. T. Kung. The final award selection was made by a committee composed of Patrick C. Fischer, Michael R. Garey (Chairman), Susan L. Graham, James Gray, Robert R. Korfhage, and Robert W. Taylor.

The committee judged this thesis to be an outstanding contribution to an important new area of computer science. The subject is the design and analysis of very large scale integrated circuits. Two particularly noteworthy contributions are made in the thesis. The first is a uniform framework for studying chip layouts within which various theoretical results are proved that justify certain heuristic techniques used in practice. The second is the development of so-called systolic architectures for simply and efficiently realizing computational algorithms as integrated circuits.

The thesis is an excellent blend of theoretical and practical concerns. Moreover, it describes this work in a clear, well-organized, and eminently readable fashion.

WALTER M. CARLSON
Chairman, ACM Awards Committee

Contents

Figures and Tables

Area-Efficient VLSI Computation

Introduction

The remarkable advance of very large scale integrated (VLSI) circuitry has sparked research into the design of algorithms suitable for direct hardware implementation. To the computer theorist, VLSI provides attractive models of parallel computation for three reasons. First, the number of electronic components that can fit on a single chip is large, and beyond that has been doubling every two years. It is currently possible to place 10^5 components on a single chip, and it is projected that this number will very likely grow to 10^7 or even 10^8. These large numbers make asymptotic analysis and other theoretical tools applicable to this engineering discipline. Secondly, VLSI hardware expense can be related directly to the very mathematical and geometric cost function of *area*. Unlike older technologies, the components and interconnections between components are made out of the same "stuff" in VLSI, and hence area is a uniform cost measure for both. Finally, VLSI provides a model of parallel computation that includes communication costs as well as operation counts. The cost of communication is represented explicitly as the area of a fixed-width wire between two processors, and the time for communication can depend on the distance between two processors. In fact, communication can consume most of the area of an integrated circuit chip and most of the computation time as well. A major goal, therefore, is to design algorithms which are both time-efficient and area-efficient using complexity measures that reflect the true implementation costs.

The two parts of this thesis address these two measures of efficiency. Part I analyzes *systolic systems* [20, 21] which marry the ideas of pipelining and multiproc-

1

essing in a single framework of design. Part II looks at the layout of their communication paths. Although the two parts fit together, it should be understood that the ideas in each stand alone. The results of Part I can be applied to systems which are not systolic, and even systems which are not assembled on integrated circuits. The layout results of Part II can be applied to more general communication structures than graphs of systolic systems, and the ideas for representing layouts can be used in other routing algorithms.

PART I

SYSTOLIC SYSTEMS

CHAPTER 1

What is a Systolic System?

1.1 Introduction

The complexity of integrated-circuit chips being produced today makes it feasible to build inexpensive, special-purpose subsystems that rapidly solve sophisticated problems on behalf of a general-purpose host computer. Of the many ways to exploit the burgeoning technology, *systolic systems* have especially desirable properties from both engineering and mathematical standpoints. Systolic systems are an attempt to capture the concepts of parallelism, pipelining, and interconnection structures in a unified framework of mathematics and engineering. They embody engineering techniques such as multiprocessing and pipelining together with the more theoretical ideas of cellular automata and algorithms, and therefore are an excellent subject for investigation from a combined standpoint.

The term "systolic" comes from "systole," which means "contraction," and in physiology refers to the contraction of the heart that drives blood through the circulatory system of the body. In a systolic system, the processors are hearts that pump multiple streams of data throughout the system. The regular beating of these parallel processors maintains a constant flow of data through the network. This "blood pressure" is the principal attribute of a systolic system. Every processor computes on each clock tick. As a processor pumps data items through itself, it performs a quick operation which may update some of the items. All operands for a computation arrive at a processor simultaneously. No waiting is necessary—the processors just compute, rhythmically and perpetually.

The central issue in parallel systems is communication, and systolic systems address this problem explicitly. Two processors that communicate must have a data path between them, and free global communication is disallowed. The farthest a datum can travel in unit time is from one processor to an adjacent processor.

Systolic systems are not general-purpose computing engines. A systolic computing system is a subsystem that performs its computations on behalf of a *host*. For example, Figure 1–1 illustrates how a special-purpose systolic device might form part of a computer system. The host need not be a computer, however. It might be a real-time data stream, or some other electronic system.

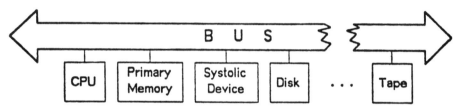

Figure 1–1: A systolic device connected to the bus of a computer system.

Many readers will see similarities between the systolic paradigm and other computational models in the literature. For instance, Stone's algorithm for performing the FFT on a *shuffle-exchange* network [37] is systolic—although communication with a host is not considered. Much study has centered on the subclass of systolic systems called *iterative arrays* [16] (also called *cellular automata* or *tesselation automata*), whose machines form a *d*-dimensional mesh. This thesis uses the name *systolic arrays* for these systems, not to add to confusion, but because they constitute the array-structured subclass of all systolic systems. The theorems of Chapter 2 will demonstrate common attributes of all systolic systems.

This is not to say that all systolic systems are created equal. VLSI technology has made one thing quite clear: simple and regular interconnections have substantial advantages over complicated interconnections. The results of Part II show that high density of processors is an immediate by-product of simple connections between processors. And technologists know that high density implies both high performance and low overhead for support components. (Sutherland and Mead [38] have a good discussion on the importance of having simple and regular geometries for processors.) Because of their regular structure, extra attention will be paid to systolic arrays and systolic trees.

The remainder of this chapter contains background and definitions and is organized as follows. Section 1.2 gives an example of a real-time systolic priority queue in order to further the reader's intuition about systolic systems. Section 1.3 discusses finite-state automata which are the basic component of systolic systems. Section 1.4 gives a formal definition for systolic systems and the related *semisystolic systems*.

1.2 A Simple Systolic Priority Queue

Before we begin a formal treatment of systolic systems, it is worthwhile to consider an example. Many programming applications require the ability to insert *records* into a set, and at any time to retrieve from the set the record having the smallest *key* according to some linear ordering. Any data structure that provides such services is called a *priority queue* [1]. The operation INSERT(Q, a) replaces the set Q with the set $Q \cup \{a\}$. The operation EXTRACTMIN(Q) returns the smallest element a of Q and replaces Q with $Q - \{a\}$.

Priority queues are usually implemented in software, but a priority queue can be built in hardware as a systolic array. One method uses identical processors, each of which is capable of sorting three elements. The *three-sorter* has three inputs X, Y, and Z and produces three outputs X', Y', and Z' which are the minimum, median, and maximum of the inputs. Table 1–2 shows this relationship between inputs and outputs. The outputs of the three-sorter are latched, and the logic is clocked so that

Table 1-2: Definition of the three-sorter.

Inputs			Outputs		
X	Y	Z	X'	Y'	Z'
x	y	z	$\min(x, y, z)$	$\mathrm{med}(x, y, z)$	$\max(x, y, z)$

when several of these processors are interconnected, the changing output of one will not interfere with the input to another. It is possible to view the processors as being asynchronous—each computes its output values when all its inputs are available. The synchronous approach adopted here is more intuitive for the results of this thesis, however, and global clocking simplifies hardware design. The issue of clocking will be discussed in more detail in Section 1.4.

Figure 1-3 shows how three-sorters are interconnected to make a systolic priority queue. In the figure, the outputs from the top, middle, and bottom of a processor are respectively the minimum, median, and maximum of the inputs. The minimum from each processor is fed leftward, and the median and maximum are fed rightward. This tends to keep smaller elements on the left and larger ones on the right. An *infinity key* ∞ which is larger than all other keys is provided as constant input on the right. The two inputs on the left are connected to the host computer. Initially, all the elements in the queue have a key of ∞. As elements are inserted on the left, they move rightward displacing ∞ keys which are output on the right. If ever the outputs on the right are not ∞'s, the queue overflows.

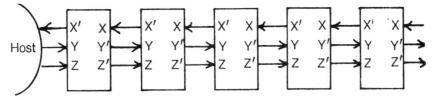

Figure 1-3: A real-time systolic priority queue.

Several steps of the operation of the systolic priority queue are illustrated in

Figure 1–4. The figure shows the data on the wires between processors. The first column shows the communication between the host and the first processor on successive clock ticks, the second column shows the communication between the first processor and the second processor, and so forth. On the first clock tick, the host inserts the item 6 into the queue by providing 6 and $-\infty$ as inputs. The first processor sorts these two values and the value -5 it receives from the second processor, and on the second clock tick outputs $-\infty$ which is ignored by the host.

Notice that on the first clock tick only odd-numbered processors do useful work, and on the second clock tick only even-numbered processors do useful work. This phenomenon occurs often in the design of systolic systems, and is the inevitable result of certain design techniques (see Chapter 2). There are several ways to achieve full utilization, however. For instance, one can coalesce adjacent processors so that only half the number are needed. Alternatively, if the number of processors is odd, the outputs from the ends of the systolic array can be piped back through the systolic array to make use of the processors which operate on the off-beat. Other variations will be discussed in future chapters.

The host performs abstract INSERT and EXTRACTMIN operations, but the basic operation of the systolic priority queue is somewhat different. With each clock tick, the systolic array performs a combination of two INSERT operations and one EXTRACTMIN. To perform an insertion of an item a on behalf of the host, the item a and a dummy $-\infty$ key are presented as input to the leftmost processor. When the clock ticks, the dummy $-\infty$ is returned as output, and the item a is inserted. The host need not be aware of the existence of the dummy $-\infty$ key, however. To perform an EXTRACTMIN operation on behalf of the host, two dummy ∞ keys are input, and after the clock ticks, the minimum element of the queue is output and returned to the host. The two dummy ∞ keys will find their way rightward in the systolic array and eventually will be output on the right, much as corn goes through the new maid. With each pair of clock ticks, the priority queue is ready to execute another INSERT or EXTRACTMIN.

	c1	c2	c3	c4	c5	c6
		−5	·	∞	·	∞
INSERT 6	6	·	−2	·	∞	·
	−∞	·	4	·	∞	
	−∞	·	−2	·	∞	·
	·	−5	·	4	·	∞
	·	6	·	∞	·	∞
	·	−5	·	4	·	∞
EXTRACTMIN	∞	·	−2	·	∞	·
	∞	·	6	·	∞	·
	−5	·	−2	·	∞	·
(−5)	·	∞	·	4	·	∞
	·	∞	·	6	·	∞
	·	−2	·	4	·	∞
INSERT 3	3	·	∞	·	6	·
	−∞	·	∞	·	∞	·
	−∞	·	4	·	6	·
	·	−2	·	∞	·	∞
	·	3	·	∞	·	∞
	·	−2	·	6	·	∞
EXTRACTMIN	∞	·	3	·	∞	·
	∞	·	4	·	∞	·
	−2	·	3	·	∞	·
(−2)	·	∞	·	4	·	∞
	·	∞	·	6	·	∞

Figure 1-4: The operation of the systolic priority queue.

It may take an element a long time to find its place in the systolic array, but to the host computer, an INSERT operation appears to take only two clock cycles. Since the minimum element in the queue is always at the left, an EXTRACTMIN operation also takes constant time. The operation of the systolic array is pipelined so that no degradation occurs even when the host executes many priority queue requests in a row. Thus we may say that the systolic array, whose *response time* is constant relative to the length of the array, exhibits *real-time* response to the operations INSERT and EXTRACTMIN.

1.3 Finite-State Automata

A systolic system is a synchronous network of parallel processors. Each processor in a systolic system is composed of a constant number of *state-output* finite-state automata which are called *Moore machines* [31]. This type of finite-state machine has the property that its outputs are dependent upon its state but not upon its inputs. The output of a *transition-output* finite-state automaton or *Mealy machine* [30], on the other hand, is a combinational function of both the state and the input. *Semisystolic systems* may contain both Moore and Mealy machines. This section explores the differences between these formulations of finite-state automata.

Figure 1–5 shows the two types of automata. Each is composed of some purely combinational logic and some clocked state. But whereas the output of the Moore machine is dependent only on the state of the machine, the output of the Mealy machine may be dependent also on the current input.

To be mathematically precise, a Moore machine is a quintuple $(Q, I, O, \delta, \lambda)$, where

- Q is a finite set of *internal states,*

- I is a finite set of *input symbols,*

- O is a finite set of *output symbols,*

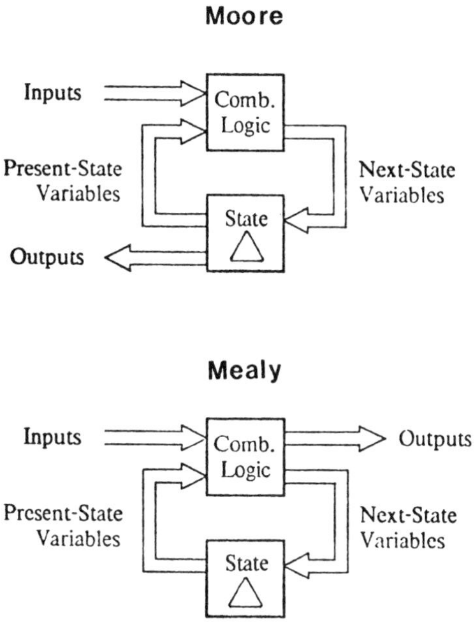

Moore

Mealy

Figure 1-5: The difference between Moore machines and Mealy machines is
where outputs are produced.

- δ, the *state transition function*, is a combinational function that maps $Q \times I$ to Q,

- λ, the *output transition function*, is a combinational function that maps $Q \times I$ to O.

In this mathematical model, *time* can be regarded an independent variable which takes on integer values and is a count of the *number* of clock cycles or state changes. The state $q(t+1)$ and output $o(t+1)$ of a Moore machine at time $t+1$ is uniquely determined by its state $q(t)$ at time t and its input $i(t)$ at time t by

$$
\begin{aligned}
q(t+1) &= \delta\big(q(t), i(t)\big), \\
o(t+1) &= \lambda\big(q(t), i(t)\big).
\end{aligned}
\tag{1-1}
$$

A *Mealy machine* is similarly defined as a quintuple $(Q, I, O, \delta, \lambda)$, where all is the same as in Moore machines except that the output at time t is dependent on input at time t, that is,

$$q(t+1) = \delta(q(t), i(t)),$$
$$o(t) = \lambda(q(t), i(t)).$$

(1-2)

These machines can be implemented in a variety of ways, all of which are consistent with the results of the next chapter. A general way to implement them on an integrated circuit, however, is with a *programmable logic array* (PLA) which has the advantage of a regular physical structure.[1] Figure 1-6 shows a PLA implementation of a Moore machine. The inputs and outputs of the "naked" PLA are clocked through the input and output registers on two phases of a clock. The state part of the output is gated out of the PLA and onto the feedback wires.

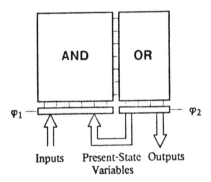

Figure 1-6: A PLA implementation of a Moore finite-state machine.

Compare this implementation of a Moore machine with a PLA implementation of a Mealy machine (Figure 1-7). The state is clocked through registers, but since the input signals are allowed to propagate through to the output unconstrained, a change in the signal on an input wire can affect the output without an intervening clock tick. When Mealy machines are strung together, signals *ripple* through the combinational logic of several machines between clock ticks. If the signals feed back on themselves before being stopped by a register, they can latch or oscillate. Even if

---

[1] The reader is referred to Mead and Conway [28] for a good description of PLA's.

the problems associated with feedback have been precluded, the settling of combinational logic can make the clock period long in systems with rippling logic. As we shall see in the next section, only Moore machines are allowed in systolic systems. The exclusion of Mealy machines helps guarantee that the clock period does not grow with system size, and makes the *number* of clock ticks be a measure of time that is largely independent of system size.

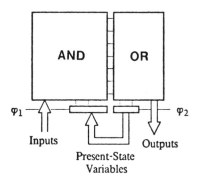

Figure 1–7: A PLA implementation of a Mealy finite-state machine.

1.4 The Systolic Model

Although a systolic system can be simply viewed as a set of interconnected Moore machines, its precise specification requires a good deal of messy notation. Instead of pursuing a course of extreme mathematical formality at the expense of the reader's intuition, we shall adopt a simplified notation. But first, it is necessary to examine what a precise notation would need to specify.

The semantics of the interconnections among many, possibly different machines are complicated. A machine v produces symbols from a set O_v as output. In the PLA implementation, this set of symbols is represented as the values of the output register. Just as this register can be divided into groups depending upon which machines the wires are connected to, so we break up each output symbol in O_v so that the pieces correspond to the *output ports* of v. Similarly, each input symbol to a machine can be apportioned among *input ports.*

In a formal specification of a connection between two machines, the machines might be vertices in a graph, and the connection an edge between them. The particular ports spanned by the connection could be designated as labels on the edge. An edge with two labels specifies the physical structure well enough, but, in addition, the semantics of the interconnection would need to be defined. We would have to say mathematically that the set of pieces of output symbols for an output port of one machine is a subset of the set of pieces of input symbols for the particular input port of the machine to which it is connected, and that the piece of input symbol from the input port is the corresponding output symbol from the other at any given time.

Rather than keeping track of all these concerns, the simplified notation specifies only which machines are connected. The structure of interconnections is given by a directed graph whose vertices are machines. If an edge (v, w) is present in the graph, this means that some output port of machine v is connected to one of the input ports of machine w. The particular ports and the symbols communicated between machines will be treated in an informal, but precise, manner.

The structure of a *systolic system* $S(n)$ is given by a *machine graph* $G = (V, E)$ of n interconnected machines where the vertices in V represent the machines and the directed edges in E represent interconnections between the machines.[2] The machines operate synchronously by means of a common clock, and *time* in the system is measured as the number of clock cycles. All the machines in V are Moore machines with the exception of one called the *host* which can be viewed as a Turing-equivalent machine that provides input to and receives output from the systolic system. To the other machines in the system, however, the host looks like just

---

[2]Technically speaking, what we really mean is that S is a class of networks, but use of this phraseology makes for labored prose. Instead, we implicitly acknowledge presence of the class by always letting n be a free variable—"a network of n processors." The term "constant" is used for a variable which is independent of n; that is, when the same constant applies for all networks in the class.

another Moore machine, i. e., signals cannot ripple through it. Based on the machine graph, the *neighborhood* of a machine $v \in V$ is the set of machines with which it communicates:

$$\text{Neigh}(v) \;=\; \{w \mid (v, w) \in E \; or \; (w, v) \in E\}.$$

For $S(n)$ to be systolic, it is further required that the Moore machines be small in the following sense. There must exist constants c_1, c_2, c_3, and c_4 such that for all n and all $v \in V - \{host\}$,

- $|Q_v| \leq c_1$ (the number of states of a machine is bounded),

- $|I_v| \leq c_2$ (the number of input symbols for a machine is bounded),

- $|O_v| \leq c_3$ (the number of output symbols for a machine is bounded),

- $|\text{Neigh}(v)| \leq c_4$ (the number of neighbors of a machine is bounded, i. e., the graph has bounded degree).

These "smallness" conditions help guarantee that the systolic model corresponds in performance to a physical implementation. They ensure that as the size of the systolic system grows, the amount of hardware needed to implement a given machine in the system remains the same. If the logic in an individual machine were to grow with system size, the time required for the logic to settle to a stable value could depend on the size of the system. Thus the measure of time in the model— number of clock ticks—would poorly reflect the actual time required in a real implementation. With the smallness conditions, however, the amount of hardware required for each machine remains small as system size grows, and hence the time needed for a machine to change state is independent of the size of the system.

The smallness conditions go a long way toward ensuring that the number of clock cycles is a good measure of time in the systolic model. A problem arises, however, when the time required to propagate a signal between machines becomes longer than the time required for the longest combinational-logic delay through a machine. The period of the clock must be at least as long as the longest propagation delay between machines, which means that the independence of the clock period from system size will not be realized for systems with long interconnections. Fortunately, this effect is relatively unimportant for many integrated circuit technologies because propagation delay is typically much shorter than switching delay. The degree to which the switching delay dominates propagation delay is a measure of the success of the model. Future work will treat models which include propagation delays.

Systolic arrays, which have only nearest-neighbor connections, are especially attractive for VLSI because propagation delay is insignificant. For this reason, they form the basis of many of the algorithms in Chapter 3 and Chapter 4. Although the interconnections in tree layouts are not nearest-neighbor, there is good reason to believe (see Mead and Rem [29], for example) that logarithmic performance can be realized for integrated circuit structures based on trees. Because of their robustness with regard to propagation delay, the results of the next chapter—though applicable to any systolic structure—are applied principally to systolic arrays and systolic trees.

The independence of clock period from the delay caused by many stages of combinational logic is invalidated when Mealy machines are allowed in a system. Despite the potential for rippling of signals from input to output to input to output, it is often easier to design with Mealy logic because global communication can be expressed so easily. For instance, *broadcasting,* the most common means of global communication, can be implemented by letting a signal ripple throughout the system until it reaches all processors.

A *semisystolic system* is exactly like a systolic system except that some of the machines may be Mealy machines. All other requirements of systolic systems apply to semisystolic systems, but in addition, the output edges from Mealy machines may not form a cycle in the machine graph. This constraint precludes the problems of unclocked state and oscillation which are associated with feedback. No such requirement is needed for the output edges from Moore machines in a semisystolic system because a changing input to a Moore machine cannot affect its output.

In a semisystolic system the outputs of a machine can be used to identify it as being Moore or Mealy. We shall adopt a graphical notation in which edges of the machine graph that originate from Moore machines are represented by double arrows $\Rightarrow$ and edges from Mealy machines are represented by single arrows $\rightarrow$. When communication goes both ways between two Moore machines, a double-headed double arrow $\Leftrightarrow$ is used.

To illustrate this notation Figure 1-8 shows a semisystolic system in which the Mealy machines (circles) implement a broadcast to the Moore machines (squares). For this example, the combinational logic in the Mealy machines is simple—a wire from the input to the outputs. Among the relationships between machines, we have that $v_1 \Leftrightarrow v_3$ and $v_4 \rightarrow v_3$. Sometimes to indicate that a machine is Mealy or Moore without specifying the machine to which the outputs go, we write $v \rightarrow$ or $v \Rightarrow$.

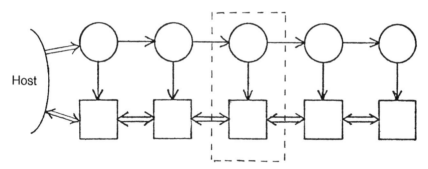

Figure 1-8: Broadcasting can be implemented by Mealy machines.

Although the machine graph gives the computational structure for a systolic or semisystolic system, it is often useful to organize groups of machines into *processors*. For the broadcasting example in Figure 1-8, each Moore machine and the corresponding Mealy machine that provides its broadcast input can be viewed as a single processor. Thus although the machine graph for this semisystolic system is a two-by-n mesh, the system could also be considered as a one-by-n linearly connected array of processors. Depending upon the logical structure of the system, one grouping might be preferred; for all but trivial systems, however, several groupings are sure to exist.

Definition: An undirected, bounded-degree graph H is a *processor graph* for a systolic or semisystolic system S with machine graph G of n vertices if there exists a constant c independent of n, and a *processor mapping* θ from the vertices of G (machines) to the vertices of H (processors) such that

- if $(v, w) \in G$, then either $\theta v = \theta w$ or $(\theta v, \theta w) \in H$, and

- if $w \in H$, then $|\{ v \mid w = \theta v \}| \leq c$.

In other words, the processor mapping θ tells which machines compose which processors. Two machines which are connected must either be in the same processor or be in adjacent processors according to the machine graph. To make sure that the size of a processor is independent of system size, at most c machines in the machine graph may be mapped to the same processor.

When the processor mapping θ is a bijection, each processor is composed of exactly one machine. The processor graph H represents the symmetric closure of G, and is called the *standard processor graph* for systolic system S. If H is the standard processor graph for a systolic system S, and H is also a processor graph for another system S', then it follows that every processor graph for S is a processor graph for S'.

CHAPTER 2

The Structure of Systolic Systems

2.1 Introduction

One problem with designing large parallel systems is the difficulty in making every processor do exactly the right thing at the right time. This problem is exacerbated for systolic systems because a processor can only communicate with adjacent processors. Data must propagate through the interconnection network, which means that machines see the same data at different times. Global control can reduce the complexity of the design task because it is often easy to think of all machines acting in unison. But global control potentially involves communication over large distances and thus can be expensive in terms of system performance. It make sense, therefore, to determine how systems specified with global communication can be implemented with local communication.

In Section 1.4, we saw an example (Figure 1-8, page 17) where broadcasting was expressed in terms of the Mealy logic in a semisystolic system. As another example of *global computation,* the host might want to retrieve information about the machine states of all the processors. For instance, the host might want to know whether every processor has a zero in some register. Still another kind of global computation is displayed by the propagation of a carry signal down the length of a simple binary counter. It is well known that *pipelining* can remove the global communication necessary for these computations in linearly connected systems with unidirectional communication, but a penalty proportional to the length of the pipeline is paid in response time. In this chapter, we show that global communication can often be removed with little expense in hardware, throughput, or response time.

For a systolic subsystem, the principal performance metrics of response time and throughput must be determined relative to the host. For instance, it is possible for an individual processor in the system to see slow response from the rest of the system, while the system nonetheless responds quickly to the host. We shall always adopt the point of view of the host because the host is interested only in the external behavior of the subsystem.

Throughput is a measure of how much work a system can do in unit time. Since time in a systolic system is measured as clock ticks, throughput will usually be expressed as a fraction of one. The systolic system may *multiplex* its activity among several independent jobs in order to increase its throughput. For example, the priority queue from Section 1.2 can perform a priority queue operation every two clock ticks. But since there are two equivalence classes of computation in the system, two jobs could use the hardware on alternate time steps yielding a throughput of one operation per unit time. For a single job, however, we say that the *dedicated throughput* is half an operation per unit time.

Because of the timing problems associated with the rippling in semisystolic systems, they are not as desirable structures as are purely systolic systems with regard to integrated circuit implementation. But since global computations such as broadcasting can be expressed easily with Mealy machines, this chapter provides transformations that convert semisystolic systems into systolic systems. In this context, the set of semisystolic systems will be a *design space* whereas the set of systolic systems will be the *implementation space*.

If one system is "converted" to another, it is expected that the second performs the same computation as the first. In the context of systolic and semisystolic systems, the operation of the subsystem from the point of view of the host is at issue. Two subsystems are said to have the same *external behavior* if, when given the same sequence of inputs, the two subsystems produce the same sequence of outputs. The performance of the two subsystems may vary, however. Since the host can feed outputs from a subsystem back into the subsystem, to declare that two systems have the same behavior is to make a strong statement indeed.[3]

The effectiveness of the transformations in this chapter can be measured by comparing the throughput and response of the new system with that of the old. Other performance parameters are readily derived. The measurements are in terms of clock ticks, which is accurate for systolic systems, but could be a gross underestimate for semisystolic systems. Rippling of logic might require that the clock period be extremely long in order to guarantee that all signals settle to well-defined values. Remembering that semisystolic systems are the design space, the assumption that combinational rippling take zero time is conservative. A constant factor slowdown from the conversion of a semisystolic system to a systolic system will be a speedup for an actual implementation of sufficient size. The slowdowns caused by applying transformations from this chapter are never more than a factor of two.

The transformations considered here have the desirable property that they leave the basic interconnection structure of the system unchanged so that a designer can choose his interconnection scheme according to criteria outside the domain of the model without fear of it being altered. He would be unhappy, for example, if his regular mesh structure were converted into a shuffle-exchange graph which is much more difficult to lay out on silicon (see Part II). On the other hand, if the

---

[3]Chapter 4 considers matrix computations which have the attribute that the inputs from the host to one machine in the system are independent from the inputs from the host to another. This situation can be modeled by considering the results of this chapter in terms of multiple, independent hosts—a degree of flexibility not assumed here.

processor graph of the original system had an edge (v, w), it is safe to say that adding the edge (w, v) would not cause the designer intolerable anguish. Therefore, the transformations we consider also have the property that the standard processor graph of the original system is a processor graph for the transformed system (and hence any processor graph for the original system is also a processor graph for the transformed system).

The remainder of this chapter is organized as follows. Section 2.2 states and proves the *Systolic Conversion Lemma* (Lemma 2–1) which forms the basis of most of the transformations considered here. Section 2.3 gives a three-step design process based on the Systolic Conversion Lemma, which is later used in Chapter 3 to design many systolic systems. The last portion of this chapter, Section 2.4, proves the *Reset Theorem* (Theorem 2–6), which shows how any system may be effectively initialized to fixed values in constant time.

2.2 The Systolic Conversion Lemma

The transformation presented in this section can, when applicable, convert a semisystolic system into a purely systolic system with little loss of efficiency in time or area. Although it is the major result of Part I, consequences of the *Systolic Conversion Lemma* are likely to be used more often in practice. For example, the Broadcast Corollary (Corollary 2–4) from Section 2.3 shows that broadcasting can always be eliminated from an otherwise systolic system.

Lemma 2–1: (*Systolic Conversion Lemma.*) Let S be a semisystolic system, and suppose each machine v in its machine graph G can be labeled with an integer $l(v)$ such that $l(host) = 0$, and such that

- if $v \Rightarrow w$, then $l(w) - l(v)$ is -1, 0, or $+1$, and

- if $v \rightarrow w$, then $l(w) - l(v)$ is $+1$.

Then there exists a purely systolic system S' that has the same behavior as S, and whose processor graph is the standard processor graph for S. The response time (in terms of clock cycles) of S' is twice that of S, the throughput is the same, and the dedicated throughput is halved.

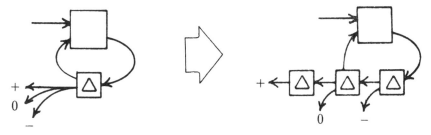

Figure 2–1: The transformation of a Moore machine in the proof of the Systolic Conversion Lemma.

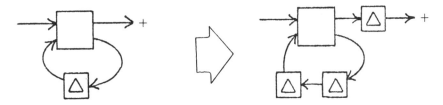

Figure 2–2: The transformation of a Mealy machine in the proof of the Systolic Conversion Lemma.

Proof. The two types of machines in S are considered separately. On the left in Figure 2–1 is a Moore machine v. The outputs that go to vertices of G labeled $l(v)-1$, $l(v)$, and $l(v)+1$ have been separated from each other. We shall adopt the notations $v \Rightarrow_- w$, $v \Rightarrow_0 w$, and $v \Rightarrow_+ w$ for each of these cases if machine w receives the output from v. In the new system S', this machine on the left in the figure is converted into the machine on the right. Figure 2–2 shows a similar conversion for the Mealy machines in S. Notice that the only outputs from the machine go to machines labeled $l(v)+1$. We adopt the notation $v \to_+ w$ if the output goes to machine w. The only difference between the old and new machines is that delays have been introduced. A unit delay has been added to change state, and various delays have been added depending upon the type of connection (see Table 2–3). Although neither of the new machines is in the form shown in Figure 1–5 for Moore machines, they are Moore machines because no outputs are dependent on the current inputs. The machine graph is the same for S' as it is for S except that all machines are Moore machines in the new system, and hence the standard processor graph for S is a processor graph for S'.

Table 2–3: Delays introduced by the Systolic Conversion Lemma.

Connection	Old Delay	New Delay
$w \Rightarrow_0 v$	1	2
$w \Rightarrow_- v$	1	1
$w \Rightarrow_+ v$	1	3
$w \to_+ v$	0	1

In order to show that the new system S' properly emulates the old, we define the *status* $s_v(t)$ of a machine v at time t in the old system S as $(q_v(t), i_v(t))$, where q_v is the present state and $i_v(t)$ is the input. These values become stable in a semisystolic system before a clock tick, and represent the inputs to the combinational logic upon which the next state depends. In the transformed system S', the input status $s_v'(t')$ of machine v at time t' is similarly defined to be $(q_v'(t'), i_v'(t'))$ which also attains stability as the inputs to the combinational logic before each clock tick.

We shall use induction to show that the status of a machine v in S' is related to the status of the corresponding machine in S by

$$s_v'(2t + l(v)) \;=\; s_v(t). \tag{2-1}$$

This invariant can easily be made to hold at some initial time. We now assume it holds for all machines at times before $t' = 2t + l(v)$ for an arbitrary machine v, and seek to show it holds for v at time t'. First, we shall show that the state portion of the status of v satisfies $q_v'(t') = q_v(t)$, and then show the corresponding result for $i_v'(t')$.

At time $2t + l(v) - 2$, the state part of the output from the combinational logic of a machine v, whether Moore or Mealy, is $q_v(t) = \delta_v(q_v(t-1), i_v(t-1))$ which is given by Equations (1-1) and (1-2). Two clock ticks will bring this value through the two delays in the state path of the transformed machine, thereby providing $q_v(t)$ as the state part of the input to the combinational logic at time t'. Thus $q_v'(2t + l(v)) = q_v(t)$ at time $t' = 2t + l(v)$.

It remains to be shown that the input part $i_v(t')$ of the status of v at time $t' = 2t + l(v)$ correctly corresponds to the outputs of other machines in S'. We consider four cases depending upon the type of interconnection between the machines in the original, semisystolic system S. In each case, we assume that (2-1) has been established for all machines in S' for times before $t' = 2t + l(v)$, and show that it holds for an arbitrary machine v at time t'.

$w =_0 v$ In the semisystolic system S, machine w is a Moore machine. The output of the combinational logic in machine w at time $t-1$ is given by Equation (1-1) as $o_w(t) = \lambda_w(q_w(t-1), i_w(t-1))$. In S, a portion of this value is provided as part of the input $i_v(t)$ to machine v at t. By the inductive hypothesis, at time $2(t-1) + l(w)$ in the new system S', the values $i_w(t-1)$ and $q_w(t-1)$ are the inputs to w. The combinational logic which implements λ_w is the same for both systems, and thus in the new system, $o_w(t)$ must be the value produced as the output of the combinational logic at time $2(t-1) + l(w)$ which equals $t' - 2$ since $l(v) = l(w)$. But in this system, the portion of $o_w(t)$ that goes to machine v must go through two delays. Thus it arrives as input to machine v at time t'.

$w \Rightarrow_- v$ As in the previous case, machine w is a Moore machine in S whose combinational logic computes $o_w(t)$ at time $t-1$, a portion of which forms part of $i_v(t)$. Since $l(v) = l(w)-1$, at time $2t+l(w)-2 = t'-1$, the inductive hypothesis states that the machine w in S′ similarly computes $o_w(t)$. This data from w goes through one delay on its way to v, so machine v correctly gets this data as input at time t'.

$w \Rightarrow_+ v$ Again a portion of the output $o_w(t)$ from a Moore machine w forms part of $i_v(t)$ in the semisystolic system S. In S′, it is computed as the output of the combinational logic in w at time $2t+l(w)-2 = t'-3$ since $l(v) = l(w)+1$. This time the data goes through three delays, so once again machine v gets the same input as it would at time t in the original system S.

$w \rightarrow_+ v$ In this case, machine w is a Mealy machine, which means that in the original system S, the output $o_w(t)$ is dependent on the inputs at time t instead of $t-1$ as is the case with Moore machines. This value is given by Equation (1–2) as $o_w(t) = \lambda_w(q_w(t), i_w(t))$. A portion of $o_w(t)$ is provided as part of $i_v(t)$. By the inductive hypothesis, the combinational logic in machine w in the systolic system S′ gets $q_w(t)$ and $i_w(t)$ as its inputs at time $2t+l(w)$ which equals $t'-1$ since $l(v) = l(w)+1$. The output $o_w(t)$ from the combinational logic goes through one delay, thus providing input to v at time t'.

This case analysis completes the proof of Lemma 2–1. □

Figure 2–4 shows a labeling for the system from Figure 1–8 that satisfies the conditions of the Systolic Conversion Lemma. Each Moore or Mealy machine has been labeled with $l(v)$ so that the conditions of the Systolic Conversion Lemma are satisfied. The transformed systolic system will have a response time which is double in terms of clock ticks. In the original semisystolic system, however, signals must ripple the length of the system in a single clock period. In the systolic system the signals ripple only through a single machine. The performance of the systolic system is better, therefore, because the clock period of the semisystolic system is many times longer.

Table 2–5 shows the transformation in tabular form. The vertical axis is the

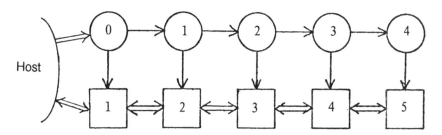

Figure 2–4: A labeling for the system from Figure 1–8 that
satisfies the conditions of the Systolic Conversion Lemma.

time t' in the systolic system S', and the horizontal axis is $l(v)$. The entries of the
table give the value of t in the semisystolic system S that a machine v with label $l(v)$
simulates in the systolic system S' at time t'. Thus, for example, at time 17 in system
S', a machine v with label 3 has status $s_v(7)$ because $17 = 2 \cdot 7 + 3$. In system S' the
value input to v is possibly dependent on the outputs of machines with label 2 at
times 14 and 16, machines with label 3 at time 15, and machines with label 4 at time
16.

Table 2–5: Comparison of timings in S and S' ($t' = 2t + l(v)$).

	-5	-4	-3	-2	-1	0	1	2	3	4	5
11	8		7		6		5		4		3
12		8		7		6		5		4	
13	9		8		7		6		5		4
14		9		8		7		6		5	
15	10		9		8		7		6		5
16		10		9		8		7		6	
17	11		10		9		8		7		6
18		11		10		9		8		7	

The state of a transformed machine goes through an extra delay from the time
it is output from the combinational logic until it is once again input. Thus there are

two distinct portions of the state of a new machine, and two clock ticks are required in the transformed system to simulate one in the old. Even though there is multidirectional communication in the system, the host sees only this slight timing change. All inputs to a machine arrive at precisely the right instant.

The two stages of machine state form two equivalence classes of computation in the new system, which leads to a halving of dedicated throughput and a doubling of response time. By multiplexing the host's interactions between two independent tasks, however, the throughput of S' can be made identical to that of S in terms of clock ticks. Thus, in terms of clock cycles, the penalty for the conversion is minimal. But since rippling is eliminated, the advantage of the systolic implementation accrues as the system size grows.

In terms of the PLA implementations of Moore and Mealy machines given in Figures 1–6 and 1–7, the extra delays can be implemented with additional registers. Since area of the combinational logic typically dwarfs the area of registers, the overhead for this conversion is minimal. For implementations of finite-state automata where most of the state is static and only a few state variables are operated on in a clock cycle, it may not be reasonable to keep two equivalence classes of computation in the system. Instead, the static memory can be clocked every other clock tick, and a delay added to the state output. The throughput will, of course, be halved.

2.3 Design Implications of the Systolic Conversion Lemma

If the stated conditions of Lemma 2–1 are satisfied, a semisystolic system can be transformed into a systolic system. From an engineering point of view, it is important to know how to design semisystolic systems that satisfy the conditions. This section provides a three-step design procedure that produces machine graphs that can be labeled so that the Systolic Conversion Lemma can be applied. The theorems of this section and the results of Section 2.4 constitute a bag of tricks that will be used for systolic algorithm design in Chapter 3.

The three-step design procedure explored in this section starts with a systolic system that performs some important piece of the desired computation. The processors in this systolic system are then augmented with Moore and Mealy machines whose interconnections follow those in the standard processor graph, which yields an intermediate semisystolic system. Finally, the Systolic Conversion Lemma is applied to the intermediate system to produce a systolic system whose processor graph is the standard processor graph of the original system.

We now investigate how the intermediate semisystolic system can be designed so that the conditions of the Systolic Conversion Lemma are satisfied. But first, we define the form of this system more precisely.

> **Definition:** Let S be a systolic system with machine graph G and standard processor graph H. A semisystolic system S$'$ with machine graph G' and processor mapping θ from G' to the same processor graph H is an *augmented systolic system based on S* if
>
> - G is a subgraph of G',
>
> - θ when restricted to the set of Mealy machines is one-to-one,
>
> - if $v \to w \Rightarrow$ in G', then $\theta v = \theta w$.

The first requirement of this definition says that S$'$ indeed augments S because the machine graph of the new system subsumes the machine graph of the old, and the second precludes two Mealy machines from belonging to the same processor. The third condition says that a Mealy machine whose output goes to a Moore machine must belong to the same processor as that Moore machine. A Mealy output can go to a Mealy machine in another processor, however.

The next theorem provides a basis for the three-step design procedure. It shows how the semisystolic system from the second step can be designed as an augmented systolic system in such a way that the third step, application of the Systolic Conversion Lemma, will always succeed. The labeling $h(\theta v)$ in the statement of the theorem is the height of θv in a breadth-first spanning forest of the processor graph H with roots in the set U.

Theorem 2-2: Let S be a systolic system with machine graph G, and let θ be the mapping from G to the standard processor graph H. Let U be an arbitrary set of processors in H, and define $h(\theta v)$ for a processor θv in H to be the length of the shortest path from θv to any element of U.

Suppose S' is an augmented system based on S with machine graph G' and mapping θ' from G' to H such that $v \rightarrow w \rightarrow$ only if $h(\theta'v) = h(\theta'w) - 1$. Then there exists a purely systolic system S'' with processor graph H whose behavior is the same as the augmented system S'. The response time of S'' is twice that of S', the throughput is the same, and the dedicated throughput is halved.

Proof. Any labeling of vertices which is given by the height of a vertex in a breadth-first spanning forest of an undirected graph satisfies the property that the label of two adjacent vertices differs by at most one. Label each Moore machine in S' with $l(v) = h(\theta'v) - h(\theta'host)$ and each Mealy machine with $l(v) = h(\theta'v) - h(\theta'host) - 1$. The label of the host is zero. Since $v \Rightarrow w$ implies v and w are either mapped to the same processor or adjacent processors in H, the first itemized condition of the Systolic Conversion Lemma holds. In the first case $v \Rightarrow_0 w$, and in the latter either $v \Rightarrow_- w$ or $v \Rightarrow_+ w$. If $v \rightarrow w \Rightarrow$, then because S' is augmented, $h(\theta'v) = h(\theta'w)$ and $v \rightarrow_+ w$. On the other hand, if $v \rightarrow w \rightarrow$, by construction $v \rightarrow_+ w$. All the conditions of the Systolic Conversion Lemma are satisfied. $\square$

Intuitively, the Mealy edges go outward from the processors in U. A dual result applies when all Mealy edges go inward toward U.

Theorem 2-3: Let S be a systolic system with machine graph G, and let θ be the mapping from G to the standard processor graph H. Let U be an arbitrary set of processors in H, and define $h(\theta v)$ for a processor θv in H to be the length of the shortest path from θv to any processor in U.

Suppose S$'$ is an augmented system based on S with machine graph G' and mapping θ' from G' to H such that $v \to w \to$ only if $h(\theta'v) = h(\theta'w)+1$. Then there exists a systolic system S$''$ with processor graph H whose behavior is the same as the augmented system S$'$. The response time of S$''$ is twice that of S$'$, the throughput is the same, and the dedicated throughput is halved.

Figure 1-8 (page 17) shows how a systolic array can be augmented with Mealy logic that implements a broadcast from the host. The Mealy edges in the machine graph of this system go outward from the host in a breadth-first manner, and therefore Theorem 2-2 can be applied to remove the Mealy rippling. In fact, any systolic system can be augmented to implement broadcasting from the host so that Theorem 2-2 is satisfied. The *Broadcast Corollary* is the single most useful consequence of the Systolic Conversion Lemma.

Corollary 2-4: (*Broadcast Corollary.*) Let S be a systolic system with standard processor graph H, and suppose that S is modified so that at any time t the host may broadcast a symbol which is provided as part of the input $i_v(t)$ to each machine in S. Then there exists a systolic system S$'$ with processor graph H whose behavior is the same as S with broadcast. The response time of S$'$ is twice that of S, the throughput is the same, and the dedicated throughput is halved.

Proof. Augment S with Mealy machines whose outputs run outward from the host in a breadth-first spanning tree. The Mealy edges so constructed satisfy the constraint that if $v \to w \to$, then the depth of v in the spanning tree is one less than the depth of w. Let the set U in Theorem 2-2 contain only the host, and apply the theorem. □

Corollaries can be obtained for other global computations, but for most applications it is easy enough to design the particular Mealy logic to run either outward or inward in a breadth-first manner and then simply apply Theorem 2–2 or Theorem 2–3. We shall see many examples in Chapter 3.

2.4 The Reset Theorem

The final result of this chapter is a theorem about resetting the states and outputs of machines in a semisystolic system to predefined values. The transformed system will itself be a semisystolic system which, if the original system satisfied the conditions of the Systolic Conversion Lemma, will itself satisfy the conditions. The reason for gearing this result toward semisystolic systems instead of systolic systems is so that it can be applied independently from the Systolic Conversion Lemma and its consequential theorems.

In order to prove the Reset Theorem, we shall need a result about semisystolic systems which is similar to one that Cole [9] proved for multidimensional systolic arrays.

> **Lemma 2–5:** Let S be a semisystolic system with machine graph G. Define $h(v)$ to be the shortest weighted path in G from the host to v where Moore edges have weight 1 and Mealy edges have weight 0. Then the state of machine v at time t is independent from any of the outputs of the host at times $t_0, t_0 + 1, \ldots, t$ if $t < t_0 + h(v)$.

Proof. Definitions (1–1) and (1–2) show that the state of any machine v at time t is determined by its inputs at time $t-1$. Thus the state of v at time t is only affected by the state of a machine w at time $t-1$ if there exists a (possibly empty) set of machines $u_1, u_2, \ldots, u_k$ such that either $w \Rightarrow u_1 \rightarrow u_2 \rightarrow \ldots \rightarrow v$ or $w \rightarrow u_1 \rightarrow u_2 \rightarrow \ldots \rightarrow v$. The label $h(v)$ of machine v must satisfy $h(v) \leq h(w)+1$ since there is at most one Moore edge between the two machines. Since the host is labeled 0, any machine whose state is affected in one time step by the output from the host at time t_0 can have label at most 1, in two time steps at most 2, etc. By induction, the state at time t of a machine v with label $h(v)$ cannot be affected by the output of the host at time t_0 unless $t \geq t_0 + h(v)$. Therefore, if $t < t_0 + h(v)$, the outputs of the host at times $t_0 + 1$, $t_0 + 2, \ldots, t$ cannot affect the state of v at time t. $\square$

A reset operation can be added to a semisystolic system by making minor changes to the Mealy and Moore machines in the system. Each machine is given an additional RESET input which affects the state and output of the machine in the following way. If the boolean signal RESET goes high at time t, the state of a machine v assumes a predefined value $\hat{q}_v$ at time $t + 1$. If v is a Moore machine, the output also assumes a predefined value $\hat{o}_v$ at time $t + 1$. But if it is a Mealy machine, the output assumes the value $\hat{o}_v$ at time t.

For the PLA implementation of Moore and Mealy machines, the addition of reset logic to a machine can be accomplished either by making changes to the PLA logic or through the use of a two-input *multiplexor*. The multiplexor takes two inputs X and Y and a boolean control signal, and produces either X or Y depending on the value of the control signal, that is, the output is $(X \wedge \neg RESET) \vee (Y \wedge RESET)$. The state and output of a machine can thus be reset by feeding the normal outputs from the PLA into X, the predefined values into Y, and then letting the RESET signal control the multiplexor.

Suppose it is desired that all machines in a semisystolic system be reset on command from the host. If the system is systolic, a global RESET signal can be broadcast to all machines from the host, and then Corollary 2-4 applied to yield a new systolic system which implements the broadcast. If the system is not systolic, however, this approach will not work unless all Mealy logic in the system goes the same direction as the broadcast. The next theorem shows, however, that any semisystolic system can be reset. Furthermore, no penalty need be paid in terms of clock ticks as it might be if Corollary 2-4 were applied.

Theorem 2–6: (*Reset Theorem.*) Let S be a semisystolic system with machine graph G and standard processor graph H, and suppose every machine v in S has a RESET input. Then there exists another semisystolic system S' with machine graph G' and processor graph H whose behavior is the same as S with global reset. The response time, throughput, and dedicated throughput of S' are all the same as S, and any labeling for G based on the Systolic Conversion Lemma can be extended to G'.

Sketch of proof. Consider H as a symmetric directed graph, and assign weights from $\{0, 1\}$ to the edges of H according to the following rule.

- if $v \Rightarrow w$ in G, then give $(\theta v, \theta w)$ a weight of 1,

- if $v \rightarrow w$ in G, then give $(\theta v, \theta w)$ a weight of 0, and

- if $(v, w) \notin G$ but $(w, v) \in G$, then give $(\theta v, \theta w)$ a weight of 1.

Each vertex θv of H is now labeled with $h(\theta v)$, which is defined as the minimum weighted path from θv to $\theta host$. Observe that since the edge weights are from $\{0, 1\}$, the labels of two adjacent vertices differ by at most one.

The global reset command is implemented by including machines in S' that, with each step of the clock, propagate a wavefront of RESET's along a breadth-first spanning tree of H rooted at the host. Along Moore edges the wavefront is clocked by new Moore machines. Along Mealy edges, new Mealy machines allow the wavefront to ripple. If the spanning tree goes along a a Mealy edge in the reverse direction, however, a new Moore machine clocks the wavefront. The idea is that in the system S some of the machines cannot be affected by normal operation of the host until some time after the host signals RESET. In the system S', the corresponding machines are reset later.

When the wavefront reaches a machine in S', it resets the state and output of the machine. Since time $t + h(\theta v)$ elapses between the time t that the host signals RESET and the time the wavefront reaches a machine v, however, the the state and outputs of the machine cannot be reset to $\hat{q}_v$ and $\hat{o}_v$. Instead, they must be reset to the values of the state and output of v in the original system S at time $t + h(\theta v)$. Lemma 2-5 guarantees that these values are well-defined because the weighted graph in the lemma is a subgraph of the weighted graph considered here. Thus we may define $\hat{q}_v(h(\theta v))$ and $\hat{o}_v(h(\theta v))$ as the state and output that machine v has in system S at time $h(\theta v))$ if RESET is signaled by the host at time 0, and be assured that $\hat{q}_v(h(\theta v))$ and $\hat{o}_v(h(\theta v))$ are well-defined constants which may be computed in advance. In summary, the state and output of each machine v in S' are reset by the wavefront to $\hat{q}_v(h(\theta v))$ and $\hat{o}_v(h(\theta v))$ at time $t + h(\theta v)$.

There is one more wrinkle in the construction. The wavefront partitions those machines that have been influenced by a global reset from those that have not. We must ensure, however, that the computations performed by a machine before it is reset do not influence any machines that have already been reset. The problem arises when a Moore machine v is reset at time $t + \theta v$, and its outputs go to a machine w which is reset at time $t + \theta w = t + \theta v - 1$. Then the output $o_v(t + \theta v - 1)$ from v, which is computed before v is reset, is provided as input to w at time $t + \theta v$—one clock tick after w is reset. A computation that does not reflect the reset dirties one that does.

On the next time step after being reset, the machine w expects part of $\hat{o}_v(\theta v)$ as input instead of part of $o_v(t + \theta v - 1)$. This problem is easily corrected with a multiplexor that, on the time step after a reset, provides the proper inputs to w from those Moore machines that are then being reset. No change is needed for inputs from Mealy machines because their outputs reflect the reset value immediately.

Any labeling of vertices in the original system S that satisfies the conditions of the Systolic Conversion Lemma can be extended to the new system S'. New Mealy machines are required to propagate the global RESET along already existing Mealy edges from already existing Mealy machines, but no other new Mealy machines are needed. New Moore machines are needed to propagate the wavefront along existing Moore edges and backwards along Mealy edges going to Mealy machines.

The new machines do not disrupt the processor graph, and since the only new Mealy edges follow existing Mealy edges, a labeling for machines in S can always be extended to machines in S'. □

CHAPTER 3

A Selection of Systolic Algorithms

3.1 Introduction

This chapter contains applications of the tools developed in Chapter 2. The second section expands on the systolic priority queue result of Section 1.2. Systolic counters are the subject of Section 3.3, and pattern matching and language recognition are the focus of Section 3.4. All of the algorithms in this chapter can be designed without using the results of the previous chapter, but with the Systolic Conversion Lemma, the Broadcast Corollary (Corollary 2–4), and the Reset Theorem, the construction of these systems is greatly simplified. Each algorithm is designed in the space of semisystolic systems in such a way that it can be converted into an efficient systolic system.

Although the "bag of tricks" accumulated in Chapter 2 apply to arbitrary processor graphs, the algorithms contained in this chapter are based primarily on trees and one- or two-dimensional arrays. These graphs have the important property that they require little area when laid out in the plane—an important consideration for implementation in silicon. Part II considers the layout problem in more detail.

Another property of the algorithms developed in this chapter is that they all provide quick response to the host. The utility of a subsystem can often be measured better by its response to a request than by its throughput. Classical

37

techniques such as pipelining improve throughput at the expense of response time. The advantage of the techniques developed in the previous chapter is that throughput is improved without sacrificing response. Subsystems for which throughput has been optimized without regard to response time perform well only when the granularity of problem size is sufficiently large. The applicability of the subsystem is thereby restricted to large numerical or signal-processing calculations which, though interesting in their own right (see Chapter 4), are hardly the bottlenecks in most computing environments.

Many of the subsystems developed in this chapter give *real-time response* to a service request by the host, that is, only a constant number of clock ticks are required to satisfy the request from the point of view of the host. For the example of the priority queue of Section 1.2, the INSERT and EXTRACTMIN operations gave real-time response. If all the operations of a subsystem give real-time response, we shall call it a *real-time subsystem.*

3.2 Priority Queues and Search Trees

In this section we construct a systolic priority queue similar to that of Section 1.2, but rather than designing the systolic array explicitly, we design a semisystolic array and apply the theorems from the previous chapter. We then extend this result to show how a binary search tree can be built in hardware which has logarithmic time response to FIND operations and pipelined performance. Finally, we present the *systolic multiqueue,* a device which provides real-time priority queue operations on several queues and dynamically shares processors among the queues. Incidental to the design of these algorithms, our "bag of tricks" will be enlarged.

3.2.1 Simple Priority Queues

It is not hard to make a linearly connected systolic array with broadcasting from the host implement a real-time priority queue. Queue items are kept sorted left-to-right in the array. The host talks to the left end of the array where the smallest item is kept. To insert an item a into the queue, the host broadcasts "INSERT(a)" to all the processors. Each processor compares a with the item it contains, those processors with larger items shift their data to the right, and the item drops into the right place. To remove the minimum element of the queue, the host broadcasts "EXTRACTMIN," and all processors shift their data left with the minimum element going to the host. Each of these operations can be implemented within one clock cycle. Therefore, the Broadcast Corollary converts this semisystolic system to a systolic system whose response time is only two clock cycles. The labeling $l(v)$ of a processor corresponds to the left-to-right index of the processor.

This implementation of a real-time priority queue should be compared with the one from Section 1.2. With the machinery of Chapter 2, it is easy to verify that this implementation actually works. The one from Section 1.2 works as well, but proving it is somewhat more difficult. Furthermore, the priority queue from this section is more easily embellished. For example, several kinds of deletions can be implemented. The simplest is the deletion of the smallest element greater than a broadcast item. The processors all listen to the broadcast item, and those with larger items shift them left.

Only slightly more involved is a priority queue that deletes an item *if it is present.* The problem is that the processors to the right of where the broadcast item belongs do not know whether the item is actually in the system. This obstacle can be overcome by changing the Mealy machines that implement the broadcast so that they perform a *priority broadcast.* In this modification of the standard broadcast scheme, what is broadcast to processors further down the line can be affected by processors closer to the host. The idea is that each Mealy machine from left to right checks to see whether it has the item to be deleted. If so, it deletes the item and passes a message to the processors down the line that they should shift their data left toward the host. If the item in a processor is smaller, however, the deletion request is forwarded down the line. Finally, if the item in a processor is the first one larger than the broadcast item, which means that the item to be deleted is not in the queue, the processor passes a message to this effect down the line. Since the direction of all Mealy outputs is away from the host, this augmented systolic system can be converted into a systolic system by virtue of Theorem 2–2.

A deficiency of the delete-if-present design is that the host cannot immediately know whether the item was actually present. In fact a simple information theoretic argument can show that no systolic array can give real-time response to this membership query. It is possible to report this exception at some later time, however.

Sometimes it is useful to be able to retrieve the elements that overflow when the queue gets full. By connecting the host to both ends of the array, the overflow can be retrieved. The broadcast in the simple priority queue can be implemented by Mealy machines whose outputs go from the ends of the array toward the middle. The priority broadcast in the delete-if-present priority queue can also be made to work from both ends.

3.2.2 Variable-Length Keys

A common characteristic of the real-time priority queues discussed so far is that the sort key for an item fits inside one processor. In order for the priority queues to be systolic, the key size must be constant, independent of the system size. The next priority queue we construct works for variable-length keys which are made up of *characters* and called *words*. Words are compared using standard left-to-right lexicographic order.

The priority queue is a linearly connected systolic array with priority broadcast. Each processor contains one character of a word, and a special symbol " # " is used to separate the words. The words are each stored with the most-significant character closest to the host. The response time for inserting a new word into the priority queue is linear in the length of the word and is constant for each character. The same is true for EXTRACTMIN—constant for each character in the minimum word. A DELETE operation can also be implemented with similar performance characteristics. Thus the priority queue gives real-time response for each character.

The EXTRACTMIN operation is straightforward to implement. The host broadcasts a shift-left to all processors and retrieves a character of the minimum word. The host repeats the broadcast until it receives a " # " to indicate the end of the word.

The INSERT operation is more involved. Each processor contains an upper register and a lower register. The items in the priority queue are kept in the upper registers. The host broadcasts each character in the word to be inserted most-significant (leftmost) character first. When the first character is broadcast, each processor copies its upper register into its lower register and shifts it right. As each subsequent character is broadcast, the array of lower-register values is shifted right. Within each word in the priority queue, a marker is propagated from left to right to determine which character in the word is to be compared with the broadcast character.

After the first character of the word to be inserted has been broadcast, each word in the queue can be labeled with S, M, or L depending on whether it is smaller, the same size, or larger than the word being broadcast. With each subsequent broadcast, some of the words labeled M will be distinguished as either S or L. Observe, however, that the processors containing the first word labeled L which are before the marked processor cannot know that their word has been labeled L, though processors down the line can. The marked processor of this word copies the broadcast character into its upper register. If a word with an M label is relabeled with L after a broadcast, the characters before the marked processor will have the same prefix as the broadcast word which is also the same as the previous first word labeled L. When the "#" is finally broadcast to indicate the end of the inserted word, each processor to the right of the marked processor in the first word labeled L copies its lower register into the upper. The upper registers now represent the priority queue with the broadcast word inserted. By eliminating the Mealy logic which implements the priority broadcast, the system becomes systolic.

A real-time DELETE operation can also be implemented. For this operation, the lower registers are shifted left instead of right, and the comparisons are performed on the lower registers instead of the upper. When the broadcast is complete, a suffix of the array of lower registers is copied into the upper registers.

3.2.3 Real-Time Order Statistics

The minimum of a dynamic set of linearly ordered elements with fixed-length keys is not the only order statistic which can be determined by a real-time systolic array. In fact, any set of order statistics can be maintained. For example, a systolic array can maintain the minimum, median, and maximum of a dynamic set whose operations include INSERT and DELETE.

The maximum of a set is easily maintained by a real-time priority queue almost identical to that of Section 3.2.1, except that the maximal element is kept next to the host instead of the minimal element and the sense of comparisons is inverted. Both maximum and minimum can be simultaneously determined by using two priority queues, one for minimum and one for maximum, and storing each element in both. This scheme can be modified, however, so that each element need only be stored once.

Place the two priority queues next to each other and consolidate corresponding processors into a single processor of the new system, each of the original priority queues occupying a *side* of the new systolic array. Let n be the number of items in each queue, and notice that the $\lfloor n/2 \rfloor$ items farthest from the host in the min side are duplicated by the $\lfloor n/2 \rfloor$ items nearest the host in the max side, and need not be stored in the min side. Similarly, the $\lceil n/2 \rceil$ items farthest from the host in the max side are duplicated by the $\lceil n/2 \rceil$ items nearest the host in the min side, and also need not be stored. Thus the systolic array can be considered to hold a "U" of items where the base of the U is about $\lceil n/2 \rceil$ processors from the host.

When an item is inserted, it takes its place on one side of the queue or the other, and causes the other elements on that side of the queue to slide down. If insertion of a new item should cause one side to have two more items than the other, however, the last item on that side slides across rather than down so that balance between the sides is maintained. Similarly, if deletion of an item would cause the queue to go out of balance, the last item on a side goes across. Only the processor that contains the base of the U makes the balance decision, but all processors must have this logic because any could be the base. One simple scheme only keeps a count of whether zero, one, or two items are currently stored in a processor.

By placing the base of the U at the front of the array instead of somewhere in the middle, the median of the items in the queue can be determined in constant time. The first processor keeps a count of the imbalance in the two halves, and if necessary, an item is transferred from one side to the other. By using a combination of the two techniques, all three order statistics, minimum, median, and maximum, can be simultaneously maintained. The elements in the systolic array form a W, and the host is connected to the processor at the top. This scheme can be generalized to keep any constant number of arbitrary order statistics in a linearly connected systolic array. Using a collection of arrays all of which talk to the host, any number of order statistics can be maintained with real-time response.

3.2.4 Search Trees

Thus far in this chapter we have concentrated on linearly connected systolic arrays which are among the simpler systolic structures. The systolic arrays from the previous sections which manipulate dynamic sets of objects do not perform one very important operation: MEMBER. The operation MEMBER(key) determines whether an item with key *key* is in the set. It is not hard to show with an information theoretic argument that any systolic structure based on a graph whose vertex degrees are bounded by a constant cannot give a response to this query in less than logarithmic time. In this section, we show that logarithmic response can be achieved with systolic search trees. The operation of these trees is pipelined to provide a dedicated throughput of one operation for every two cycles and by multiplexing, a throughput of one operation per cycle can be achieved.

One scheme for implementing the operations INSERT, DELETE, and MEMBER is illustrated in Figure 3-1. The processors in the systolic array are also leaves of a systolic tree. Each processor contains one item of the dynamic set, and the items are kept in sorted order left to right. The host talks to the root of the tree, and broadcasts the commands to the processors along the edges of the tree. Removing the broadcast from this semisystolic system yields a systolic system with the performance attributes stated above.

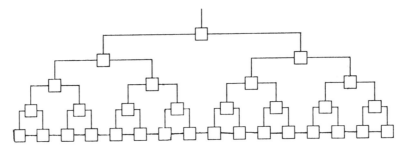

Figure 3-1: The tree-like systolic structure that performs MEMBER with $O(\lg n)$ response.

When the host requests an INSERT operation to be performed, the processors at the leaves determine whether to shift right or stay fixed, and the new item drops into place in the sorted array. For a DELETE operation, the processors again decide whether to shift right or left. Unfortunately, if the element is not in the queue, the processors making the decision as to whether to shift their contents left cannot be aware of this eventuality. We shall return to this issue shortly.

When a MEMBER operation is performed, the processor that contains the item propagates TRUE up the tree. The other processors propagate FALSE. Each internal node of the tree propagates the logical OR of its sons up to its father. After $\lg n$ time, the response to the MEMBER query is received by the host. In the meantime, if the host has been able to proceed without the response from the query, it is able to perform more operations.

The problem with deletion can be resolved using the systolic tree. Rather than deleting an object initially, a command is broadcast to mark it for deletion. A message stating whether the marking was successful is propagated up the tree. When it arrives at the root, a broadcast to garbage collect the item is made. With little additional complexity, this broadcast can be made in parallel with the broadcasts by the host. The systolic structure will never become too full with items marked for deletion because at most $\lg n$ items out of n can be so marked.

It is possible to use a complete binary tree instead of the "array-tree," and to store the items in the internal nodes of the tree as well as the leaves. To understand how this might be done, consider enveloping all the branches of the tree with a single curve as shown in Figure 3–2. Each internal node contains three items, and the curve gives the order each of the three items is visited in a tree walk. For example, the first item in node 2 is visited after the first item in node 1, the second item in node 2 is visited after the third item in node 4, and the third item in node 2 is visited after the third item in node 5. When an item to be inserted is broadcast, each node determines which way to shift the elements along the linear ordering of the curve.

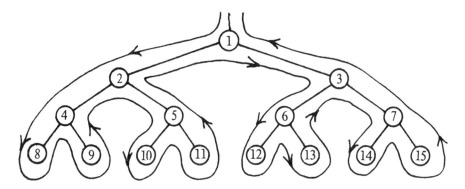

Figure 3-2: The linear ordering of a combined preorder, inorder, and postorder tree walk.

The MEMBER operation seems to cause a problem, however, because a given item may find itself at any level in the tree. If no precautions are taken, different responses may collide on their way up the tree. This difficulty can be avoided by making use of the fact that all the leaves of the tree are the same distance from the root. Mealy logic forwards the response of each internal node to the broadcast MEMBER operation down to the leaves of the tree. On the subsequent $\lg n$ time steps, the responses propagate back up to the root in a single wavefront with no possiblility of collision with responses from other MEMBER operations. Since the Mealy logic goes in the same direction as the broadcast from the root, they can both be removed to make a systolic implementation.

In either the tree or combined array-tree scheme, the MEMBER operation gives logarithmic response. The INSERT and DELETE operations, however, give real-time response, and thus the host could proceed without waiting if either of these operations were performed.

3.2.5 The Systolic Multiqueue

Suppose a computer system includes several of the simple priority queues from Section 3.2.1. Whatever the size of each, the capacity of one might be exceeded while most of the other queues are empty. This section presents a device that manages several priority queues which share a joint capacity. For any priority queue Q, the *systolic multiqueue* can perform EXTRACTMIN(Q) and INSERT(Q, a) with real-time response.

Figure 3–3 illustrates the organization of the systolic multiqueue. Each of the queues managed by this device requires a systolic-array priority queue with overflow. The host accesses any of these short systolic arrays in the normal manner, but it can access only one at a time. When a systolic array overflows, the overflow element travels through a systolic switching network to a large systolic search tree which is shared by all the queues. The item, with the queue number to which it belongs prepended to its key, is then inserted into the systolic tree which is shared by all the queues.

Besides the INSERT operation, the systolic search tree is able to remove the smallest member of any queue. This variation on EXTRACTMIN is easily implemented using the search-tree ideas from Section 3.2.4. The response from this operation will be $2 \lg n$ if the number of items that can be stored in the tree is n, but another operation can be started every two cycles.[4]

Each of the systolic arrays holds $(\lg n + \lg m)/2$ items, and performs operations on behalf of the host and on behalf of the interconnection network alternately, each operation requiring two cycles. Whenever the minimum element is removed from one of the arrays, a retrieval request goes through the interconnection network and into the systolic search tree to remove the smallest item which overflowed from that

---

[4]Although there are two equivalence classes of computation in the systolic search tree and the systolic arrays, the description here makes use of only one.

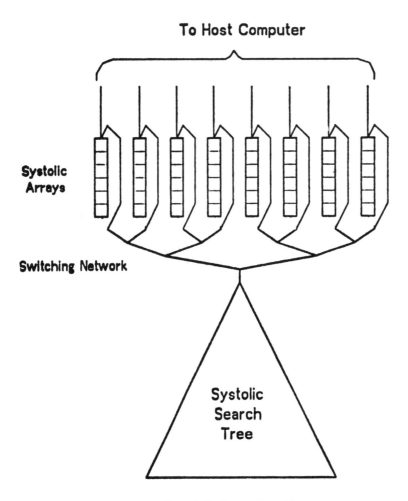

Figure 3-3: The systolic multiqueue.

queue. Items retrieved from the search tree travel back through the switching network and are inserted into the appropriate queue. Since the host may be performing insertions as well, their use of the systolic arrays must be multiplexed. The round trip time from retrieval request to insertion of an item back into the systolic array is $2(\lg n + \lg m)$.

The basic idea behind the operation of the systolic multiqueue is that each systolic array caches the smaller items in its queue. The host may attempt to exhaust the systolic array by executing $(\lg n + \lg m)/2$ EXTRACTMIN's which require

$2(\lg n + \lg m)$ cycles. But this is exactly the response time required to satisfy the retrieval resulting from the first EXTRACTMIN, and thus this item will be inserted into the systolic array in time to satisfy the $((\lg n + \lg m)/2) + 1$st EXTRACTMIN request. Moreover, the interconnection network and systolic search tree are full of a continuing stream of items which will satisfy all subsequent requests on that particular queue. It doesn't matter whether the host accesses different queues either. Each systolic array will always have the correct smallest item in it whenever the host performs an EXTRACTMIN on that queue.

The number of processors in the systolic arrays and interconnection network is $O(m \lg n)$. If the size of the systolic search tree is doubled, only $O(m)$ processors need be added to the systolic arrays. Systolic arrays with fifty processors could handle any practicable value of n.

3.3 Counters

The marker propagation used in Section 3.2.2 can be implemented by a simple shift register with exactly one bit on at any time. By connecting one end of the shift register to the other so that the marker cycles, a *ring counter* is created. Rather than having a long connection from one end of this systolic device to the other, the counter can be folded back on itself to form a U which can be embedded in a linearly connected array.

If a ring counter has n stages, it counts modulo n. Every n cycles the marker passes the host. It is not difficult to customize a modulo n ring counter so that it can count modulo m for any m that is at most n. One way is to modify the $\lceil m/2 \rceil$ processor to act as the base of the U. This change could be made off-line, but it is also possible to quickly set the modulus to any one of a constant number of values on-line by using the Reset Theorem (Theorem 2–6).

The number system which a ring counter uses is essentially unary, and thus the hardware grows proportionally with the modulus. Is it possible to build a systolic modular counter using the binary number system? The answer is yes. We present one here which is based on the *carry-save* adder [32]. This systolic-array device can reduce the sum of three binary numbers to the sum of two. Suppose at time t the processors in the array hold three n-bit numbers $x(t)$, $y(t)$, and $z(t)$. Processor i holds the ith bit $x_i(t)$ of x, the ith bit $y_i(t)$ of y is provided as input to Processor i from Processor $i-1$, and $z_i(t)$ is another input whose source will be discussed later. Each processor computes the two-bit sum:

$$x_i(t+1) + 2y_{i+1}(t+1) \; = \; x_i(t) + y_i(t) + z_i(t). \tag{3-1}$$

That $x(t+1)+y(t+1)$ equals $x(t)+y(t)+z(t)$ can be seen by multiplying both sides of (3-1) by 2^i and summing over i. The high-order bit $y_{i+1}(t+1)$ of the result is forwarded to Processor $i+1$, and the low-order bit $x_{i+1}(t+1)$ remains in Processor i. Thus the processors are ready to perform another carry-save addition in one time step.

The systolic binary counter is essentially a carry-save adder with some modifications. All values of $z_i(t)$ are zero except for Processor 0 which is next to the host and has a z input of one. After each cycle, therefore, the sum $x(t+1)+y(t+1)$ is equal to $x(t)+y(t)+1$. By throwing away the carry output of the processor containing the high-order bit, the sum is taken mod 2^n. Mealy logic running back to the host determines whether the counter is at zero. The following theorem will be used to design this Mealy logic.

> **Theorem 3-1:** Let S be a linearly connected systolic array with n processors, and let L be a regular language over the sentences of some alphabet Σ. Number each processor in order so that the processor farthest from the host is labeled 1 and the one closest to the host n, and suppose that Processor i provides a symbol a_i from Σ as an unconnected output. Then S can be augmented with Mealy logic which runs from Processor n to the host and determines for the host whether the sequence a_i, $i = 1, \ldots, n$ is a sentence in L.

Proof. The language L can be accepted by a finite automaton[5] $M = (K, \Sigma, \delta, q_0, F)$ where K is a finite, nonempty set of states, Σ is the alphabet, δ is the transition function that maps $K \times \Sigma$ to K, $q_0 \in K$ is the initial state, and $F \subset K$ is the set of final states. The ith Mealy machine in the augmented system takes as input a_i from Processor i as well as a state symbol q_{i-1} from Processor $i-1$. It performs δ on these two values and provides q_i as output to Processor $i+1$. Processor 1 has the initial state q_0 as input, and the output q_n from Processor n goes to the host. By induction $q_n \in F$ if and only if the sequence a_i is a sentence in L. □

Suppose each processor in the counter provides the two-bit sum $x_i(t) + y_i(t)$ as an unconnected output. The regular language $(1*20*)+0*$ describes the outputs (high-order to low-order) when the counter is at zero modulo 2^n. Applying first Theorem 3–1 and then Theorem 2–3 yields a systolic-array, modulo 2^n, binary counter that tells when it is at zero.

It is relatively straightforward to make this counter run modulo m for any m which is at most 2^n since a regular language can recognize when the outputs form m. For the modulo 2^n counter, the carries out of the high-order processor could be thrown away. For a general modulo m counter, however, we use the Reset Theorem to reinitialize the system so that the counting starts over anew.

Sometimes it would be useful to be able to have the counter stop counting and resume later. The systolic counter now adds one unconditionally every two clock cycles. (Two, because a consequence of the Systolic Conversion Lemma was used to construct the counter.) The host can control whether the counter counts by having it set the z input on Processor 0 to one or zero. If it is zero, the counter will continue to operate with each clock cycle, but will add zero. The carry-save additions will continue, but the sum of x and y will remain the same.

---

[5]The same construction works if M is a nondeterministic finite-state automaton. A nondeterministic implementation can often save hardware over a deterministic one.

Our last counter is a binary up-down counter.[6] Two counters of the kind just described form the upper and lower sides of a systolic array. To count up, one is added to the upper counter and zero to the lower. To count down, zero is added to the upper and one to the lower. The count does not change if zero is added to both. Mealy logic based on Theorem 3-1 tests to see whether the carry-save difference of the numbers stored in the two sides is zero.

3.4 Pattern Matching and Language Recognition

Among the applications of systolic arrays found in the literature, the problem of real-time language recognition has been addressed by several, notably Cole [9] and Foster and Kung [12]. Cole was the first to address the real-time aspect of language recoginition by iterative arrays of finite automata. In this section, two results of Cole are duplicated, and a variation on the systolic pattern matcher of Foster and Kung is presented.

The first problem due to Cole is the real-time recognition of *palindromes,* strings w such that $w = w^R$ where w^R is the reverse of w. The ith character of a palindrome, for $i = 1, \ldots, \lceil n/2 \rceil$ must be the same as the $n - i + 1$st character. Cole constructs a systolic array which is supplied characters from a string, and for each character tells immediately whether the string input up to that point is a palindrome. Whereas Cole constructs the systolic array explicitly, we are able to use the results of Chapter 2.

The host talks to one end of the systolic array, and like the priority queue and binary counter, the characters in the systolic array form a U. Characters enter on one side of the U and move down. When a character goes beyond the base of the U, it takes a permanent position on the other side so that the number of characters on

---

[6]Guibas [14] has independently designed a systolic up-down counter that informs a host when it is at zero.

each side is the same plus or minus one. Thus if n characters of a string have been input, Processor i, for $i = 1, \ldots, \lceil n/2 \rceil$, contains the ith and $n - i + 1$st characters of the string. It is a simple matter to compare the two characters in each processor and use Mealy logic which runs back to the host to answer whether the string is a palindrome. The Reset Theorem can also be applied to make the systolic array ready for another string immediately, something which Cole's device does not do.

The other problem considered by Cole is the real-time recognition of strings of the form ww, a language which is not context-free. A systolic array that can recognize this set of strings is only slightly more complicated. Like the systolic array which maintains the minimum, median, and maximum of a set, each processor contains four characters which form a W in the systolic array.

Characters are input into one end of the top of the W and come back up the corresponding U. Then they go back down the other U and find their permanent places on the other end of the W as in the palindrome recognizer. The two bases of the U's are kept the same height by transferring a character from one U to the other every two clock cycles. The processors compare the corresponding characters of the two U's, and Mealy logic determines whether the halves match.

The fabrication in nMOS of Foster and Kung's systolic pattern matcher verified the hypothesis that systolic algorithms make for high-performance and easily designed integrated circuits. A systolic array holds the pattern and compares it with a string. The pattern may contain a special *wild card* character "?" which matches any character of the string. As the string is input, the systolic array produces a string of zeroes and ones indicating where the pattern matched the string. Their pattern matcher has very high throughput—one string character per bit comparison—but the result bit corresponding to a given character of the file is delayed somewhat from the time the character is input. This delay is proportional to the sum of the length of the pattern and the number of bits per character.

The systolic pattern matcher proposed here uses a somewhat different model because we take the number of bits in a character as a constant rather than as a free variable independent of the length of the pattern. But whereas the boolean string of outputs from Foster and Kung's pattern matcher is delayed in proportion to the number of characters in the pattern, the pattern matcher here provides a response after one character comparison.

The array is loaded with the pattern so that the last character of the pattern is nearest the host. As characters from the host are input, they shift down in the array. Mealy logic running back to the host performs the comparisons between the corresponding string characters and pattern characters; the wild card "?" presents no special difficulty. The throughput of this pattern matcher is one character comparison per cycle, before the semisystolic system is converted to be systolic. Using Foster and Kung's idea of pipelining the character comparisons, a throughput of a bit comparison per cycle can be obtained with a response time proportional to the number of bits per character.

The pattern matching problem above can be solved in terms of transition diagrams of nondeterministic finite-state automata. A NFSA that recognizes a particular pattern can be built out of $n+1$ states if the pattern has n characters (see Figure 3–4). It contains an initial state and a state for each character in the pattern, the last character corresponding to the final state of the NFSA. A transition arc labeled "?" (all characters) goes from the initial state to itself. Transistion arcs labeled with characters in the pattern go sequentially from one state to the next. This NFSA can be converted directly into a semisystolic array by letting the states be one-bit processors and letting the transition arcs be wires between processors gated on the logical AND of the state bit and a comparison of the label and a broadcast symbol. By broadcasting from the final state, the host can see immediately whether the string up to this point is accepted. The Broadcast Corollary can be used to remove the broadcasting.

The direct conversion of an NFSA into an integrated circuit was proposed by

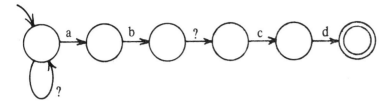

Figure 3-4: Any string ending with "ab?cd" is recognized by this NFSA.

Floyd and Ullman [11], but they do not attempt to make the implementation systolic. Using the slicing technique from Part II (obtained independently) and the McNaughton-Yamada algorithm [27] which converts a regular expression into an NFSA, they show that any language described by a regular expression of length n can be recognized by a linear area circuit.

A constant-response systolic implementation of an NFSA can sometimes be obtained by letting the host broadcast along a minimum spanning tree originating at the final states, and then removing the broadcast. Sufficient conditions on the transition diagram of an NFSA so that this will work are:

- all ε-transitions must go in the same direction as the broadcast,

- the fan-in and fan-out from a state must be bounded by a constant.

Weaker requirements may suffice, and these conditions do not give any intuition as regards which regular languages are recognizable in real-time. By implementing fan-out as a tree, the second constraint can be eliminated if logarithmic-time recognition is satisfactory. Since one cycle of a semisystolic system with n processors can always be simulated by n cycles of a similar systolic system, one interpretation of Floyd and Ullman's result is that a language described by a regular expression of length n can be recognized by a linear area systolic system whose response is n cycles. It remains to classify regular languages in terms of the response time of a systolic implementation. In all likelihood, response time will interact strongly with area.

CHAPTER **4**

Matrix Computations on Systolic Arrays[7]

4.1 Introduction

Systolic arrays are well-suited to matrix computations. In this chapter, we show that linearly connected systolic arrays can perform matrix-vector multiplication, solve triangular systems of linear equations, and compute convolutions, discrete Fourier transforms, and finite impulse response filters. Two-dimensional meshes conveniently compute matrix multiplication and the LU-decomposition of a matrix. For these last two problems, it turns out that *hexagonally mesh-connected* or *hex-connected* processors are more natural than the standard, orthogonally mesh-connected processors, and that almost exactly the same systolic array can be used for both. For all these problems, connections to the host occur only on the boundary of the particular systolic array.

The size of each of the systolic array networks is dependent only on the band width of the band matrix to be processed, and is independent of the length of the band. Thus a fixed-size systolic array can pipeline band matrices with arbitrarily long bands. The pipelining aspect of the systolic system is most effective for band matrices with long bands, of course, but since any matrix can be considered to be a band matrix with the widest-possible band, all results apply equally well to dense matrices.

---

[7]The results in this chapter were obtained jointly with my advisor, H. T. Kung, and were originally reported in [21].

Matrix computations allow a flexibility not seen in the results of the previous chapter. In general, reponse time is not as important for these problems as throughput. The host provides input and retrieves output, but rarely if ever does it alter the data provided to a subsystem as a consequence of a particular output value. And indeed, the various rows or columns of a matrix are usually independent, and thus only a predetermined order of matrix input is required, but it need not be any particular order.

The host as described in Chapter 1 placed more severe constraints on the systolic system in that it could influence the data provided to the systolic system as a result of an output from the system. When throughput is being optimized, however, each connection to the systolic system can be considered independent, and data does not reenter the system. If the system were considered to have multiple independent hosts which could be labeled differently, the results of Chapter 2 could be used to design systolic arrays for these problems. Because the systolic systems from this chapter are simple and were designed before more powerful design techniques were known, semisystolic descriptions are not given and only the systolic implementation is presented. In addition, the flow of data on these systolic arrays is aesthetically appealing.

Another feature of the problems considered in this chapter is the similarity of their computations on a standard uniprocessor. Each contains somewhere a loop that evaluates the *inner product* of two vectors:

```
FOR i _ 1 TO n DO
    InnerProduct _ InnerProduct + x[i] * y[i]
```

The repeated multiply-and-add operation in this loop is called the *inner-product step,* and it forms the basis for a processing element which we now describe. The *inner-product-step processor* has three inputs X, Y, and Z and three outputs X', Y', and Z'. Table 4–1 describes the relationship between the inputs and outputs. As is the case with all systolic processors, the inner-product-step processor is a Moore

Table 4-1: Definition of the inner-product-step processor.

Inputs			Outputs		
X	Y	Z	X'	Y'	Z'
x	y	z	x	y	$z + xy$

machine. Thus when several of these processors are interconnected, the changing
output of one will not interfere with the input to another. Figure 4-2 shows two
geometries that will be used in this chapter for the inner-product-step processor. In
type (a) geometry, which will be used in Section 4.2 for matrix-vector computations,
the Y and Z connections go horizontally in opposite directions, whereas the X
connections are vertical. Type (b) geometry, which will be used in Section 4.3, has
the X and Y connections going down to the right and left, respectively, and the Z
connection going up.

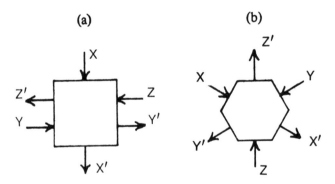

Figure 4-2: Two geometries for the inner-product-step processor.

4.2 Matrix-Vector Computations

In this section, we show how matrix-vector computations can be performed in a pipelined fashion on linearly connected systolic arrays. Multiplication of a vector by a matrix is the topic of Section 4.2.1. The systolic array which performs this computation is the basis of the other algorithms in this section. For example, triangular linear systems of equations can be solved with a similar systolic array (see Section 4.2.2). Several applications of the matrix-vector multiplication are given in Section 4.2.3.

4.2.1 Matrix-Vector Multiplication

We first consider the problem of multiplying a matrix $A = (a_{ij})$ with a vector $x = (x_1, \ldots, x_n)^\mathsf{T}$. The elements in the product $y = (y_1, \ldots, y_n)^\mathsf{T}$ can be computed by the following recurrences.

$$
\begin{aligned}
y_i^{(1)} &= 0, \\
y_i^{(k+1)} &= y_i^{(k)} + a_{ik} x_k, \\
y_i &= y_i^{(n+1)}.
\end{aligned}
\tag{4-1}
$$

Let A be an n-by-n band matrix with band width $w = p+q-1$ and let x be a vector of length n. The following equation shows an instance of the problem when $p = 2$ and $q = 3$.

$$\begin{matrix} p \\ \overbrace{\quad\quad} \end{matrix}$$

$$q\left\{\begin{bmatrix} a_{11} & a_{12} & & & & \\ a_{21} & a_{22} & a_{23} & & & 0 \\ a_{31} & a_{32} & a_{33} & a_{34} & & \\ & a_{42} & a_{43} & a_{44} & a_{45} & \\ & & a_{53} & & & \cdot \\ & & & & & \cdot \\ & 0 & & & & \cdot \end{bmatrix}\begin{bmatrix} x_1 \\ x_2 \\ x_3 \\ x_4 \\ \cdot \\ \cdot \\ \cdot \end{bmatrix} = \begin{bmatrix} y_1 \\ y_2 \\ y_3 \\ y_4 \\ \cdot \\ \cdot \\ \cdot \end{bmatrix}\right. \qquad (4\text{--}2)$$

$$\qquad\qquad A \qquad\qquad\qquad x \qquad\qquad y$$

The matrix-vector product can be computed by pipelining the elements of x and y through a systolic array which consists of w linearly connected inner-product-step processors. The systolic array that solves the instance of the band matrix-vector multiplication problem in Equation (4–2) has four inner-product-step processors and is illustrated in Figure 4–3.

The overall scheme of the computation can be viewed as follows. The y_i, which are initially zero, are move to the left while the x_i are move to the right and the a_{ij} go down. (For the general problem of computing $Ax + d$ where $d = (d_1, \ldots, d_n)^T$, each y_i should be initialized as d_i.) Each y_i accumulates all its terms, namely $a_{i,i-2} x_{i-2}$, $a_{i,i-1} x_{i-1}$, $a_{i,i} x_i$, and $a_{i,i+1} x_{i+1}$, before it leaves the network. Figure 4–4 illustrates the first seven steps in the operation of the systolic array. Although half the processors in the systolic array are idle at any given time, it is easy to coalesce adjacent processors so that only $w/2$ processors are used for a general band matrix with band width w. Alternatively, if the number of processors is odd, the outputs from the ends of the systolic array can be piped back through the

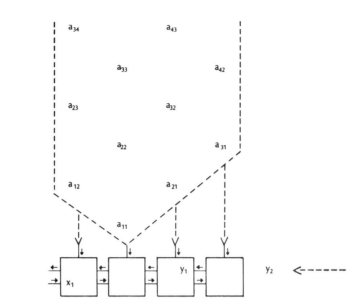

Figure 4-3: The linearly connected systolic array that performs
matrix-vector multiplication.

systolic array to make use of the processors which operate on the off-beat. There are
many other variations based on arranging the matrix and vector elements in a
different order.

If the bandwidth of A is $w = p+q-1$, after w clock ticks the components of
the product $y = Ax$ exit from the left-end processor at the rate of one every two
units of time. Therefore, the systolic network computes all the n components of y in
$2n+w$ time units, as compared to the $O(wn)$ time needed for the straightforward
sequential algorithm on a uniprocessor computer.

The number of processors required by this systolic algorithm can sometimes be
reduced if more is known about the structure of the matrix. For example, the
matrices arising from a set of finite differences or finite elements approximations to
differential equations are usually sparse band matrices which have nonzero entries
in only a few diagonals of the matrix. In this case some of the processors in the
systolic array will always receive zero values for the a_{ij}. By introducing proper

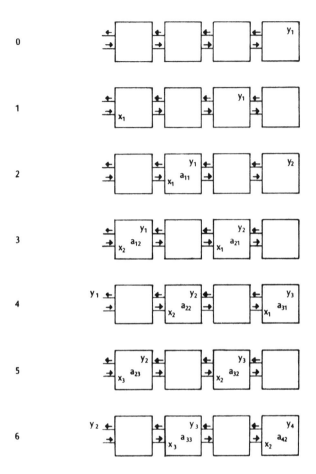

Figure 4-4: The operation of the linear systolic array in Figure 4-3.

delays between those processors that receive nonzero input, the number of processors required by the systolic array can be reduced to the number of diagonals which contain nonzero entries. This variant is useful for performing iterative methods involving sparse band matrices.

The systolic array for matrix-vector multiplication also works for dense n-by-n matrices because these are simply band matrices with the maximum possible band width. The advantage of defining the algorithms for band matrices is that the hardware requirements are proportional to the width of the band. Furthermore, if the band width of a matrix is so large that it requires more processors than a given array provides, the matrix can be decomposed into submatrices whose sizes match the size of the hardware.

4.2.2 Triangular Linear Systems

The systolic array described above computes the matrix-vector product Ax. The inverse problem is to solve for the vector x in the system of linear equations $Ax = b$. This problem is often solved by using Gaussian elimination to factor the matrix A into a lower triangular matrix L and an upper triangular matrix U, a technique called *LU-decomposition*. (We shall see in Section 4.3.2 that a two-dimensional systolic array can quickly compute the *LU*-decomposition.) After the factorization the triangular linear systems $Ly = b$ and $Ux = y$ must be solved. This task is well-suited to linearly connected systolic arrays.

Let $A = (a_{ij})$ be a nonsingular n-by-n lower[8] triangular band matrix, and let $b = (b_1, \ldots, b_n)^\mathsf{T}$ be given. The problem is to determine $x = (x_1, \ldots, x_n)^\mathsf{T}$ such that $Ax = b$. The following recurrences show how the vector x is computed by a technique known as *forward substitution:*

$$
\begin{aligned}
y_i^{(1)} &= 0, \\
y_i^{(k+1)} &= y_i^{(k)} + a_{ik} x_k, \\
x_i &= (b_i - y_i^{(i)})/a_{ii}.
\end{aligned}
\qquad (4\text{--}3)
$$

Suppose that A is a band matrix with band width $w = q$. (See Figure 4–5 for the case when $q = 4$.) Then a systolic array similar to the one used for band matrix-vector multiplication can be used to solve the forward substitution recurrences. (Observe the similarity of the defining recurrences (4–1) and (4–3) for these two

---

[8]Since an upper triangular linear system can always be rewritten as a lower triangular linear system, without loss of generality we deal with only lower triangular linear systems.

problems.) For the instance of this problem in Figure 4–5, the systolic array is shown in Figure 4–6.

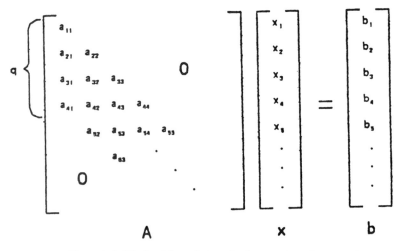

Figure 4–5: The band (lower) triangular linear system where $q = 4$.

The elements of y enter the systolic array as zero and go leftward while the elements of x, a, and b move as indicated in the figure. The processor represented as a circle is not an inner-product-step processor. It performs the operation $x_i - (b_i - y_i)/a_{ii}$. Each y_i accumulates inner-product terms as it moves through the network, one term per processor. By the time y_i reaches the division processor it has the value $a_{i1}x_1 + a_{i2}x_2 + \ldots + a_{i,i-1}x_{i-1}$, and consequently, the x_i output by this processor will have the correct value $(b_i - y_i)/a_{ii}$. Figure 4–7 gives "snapshots" of the first seven steps in the operation of the systolic array. From the figure one can check that the final values of x_1, x_2, x_3, and x_4 are all correct.

With this systolic array an n-by-n band triangular linear system with band width $w = q$ can be solved in $2n + q$ steps. As we have observed before, the number of processors required by the array can be reduced to $w/2$ or the output can be piped back through the array to achieve 100% utilization.

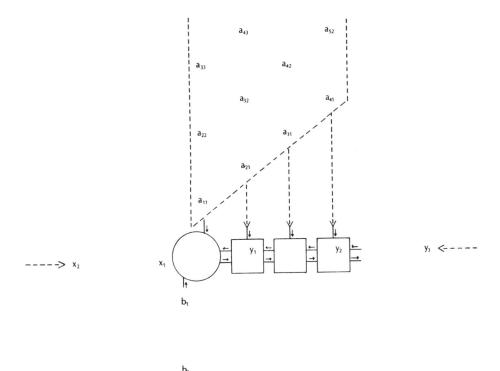

Figure 4-6: The linearly connected systolic array for solving the triangular linear system in Figure 4-5.

4.2.3 Variants of Matrix-Vector Multiplication

There are many important problems which can be formulated as matrix-vector multiplication problems and thus can be solved rapidly by the systolic array of Section 4.2.1. The problems of computing convolutions, finite impulse response (FIR) filters, and the discrete Fourier transform (DFT) are such examples.

If a matrix has the property that the entries on any diagonal parallel to the main diagonal are all the same, then the matrix is a *Toeplitz matrix*. The convolution problem is simply the matrix-vector multiplication where the matrix is a triangular

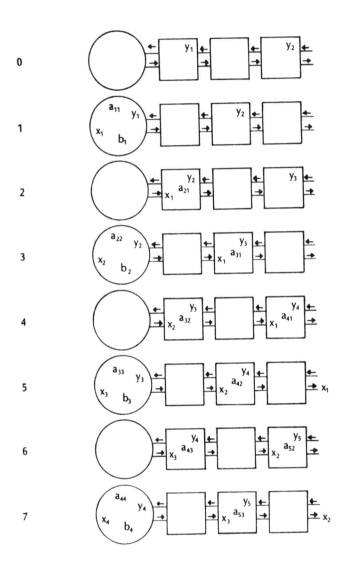

Figure 4-7: The operation of the linear systolic array in Figure 4-6.

Toeplitz matrix (see Figure 4–8). A p-tap FIR filter can be viewed as a matrix-vector multiplication where the matrix is an upper triangular Toeplitz matrix with band width $w = p$. Figure 4–9 represents the computation of a 4-tap filter. An n-point discrete Fourier transform is the matrix-vector multiplication in which the (i, j)th entry of the matrix is $\omega^{(i-1)(j-1)}$, where ω is a primitive nth root of unity. (See Figure 4–10).

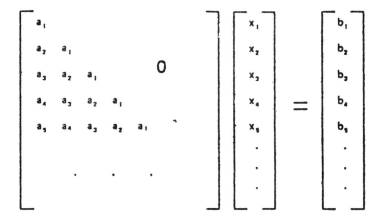

Figure 4–8: The convolution of vectors a and x.

Using a linearly connected systolic array of n processors, both the convolution of two vectors of length n and the n-point discrete Fourier transform can be computed in $O(n)$ units of time, rather than $O(n \lg n)$ as required by the sequential FFT algorithm. Observe that for the convolution and filter problems, each processor has to receive an entry of the matrix only once. This entry can be shipped to the processor through horizontal connections and stay in the processor during the rest of the computation thus obviating the need for external vertical connections.

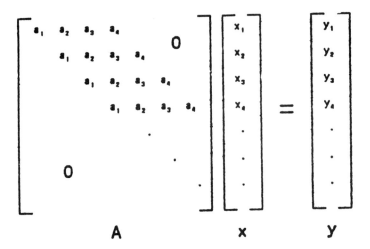

Figure 4–9: A 4-tap FIR filter with coefficients a_1, a_2, a_3, and a_4.

$$
\begin{bmatrix}
1 & 1 & 1 & 1 & 1 \\
1 & \omega & \omega^2 & \omega^3 & \omega^4 \\
1 & \omega^2 & \omega^4 & \omega^6 & \omega^8 \\
1 & \omega^3 & \omega^6 & \omega^9 & \omega^{12} \\
1 & \omega^4 & \omega^8 & \omega^{12} & \omega^{16} \\
 & & & & & \ddots
\end{bmatrix}
\begin{bmatrix}
x_1 \\ x_2 \\ x_3 \\ x_4 \\ x_5 \\ \cdot \\ \cdot \\ \cdot
\end{bmatrix}
=
\begin{bmatrix}
b_1 \\ b_2 \\ b_3 \\ b_4 \\ b_5 \\ \cdot \\ \cdot \\ \cdot
\end{bmatrix}
$$

Figure 4–10: The discrete Fourier transform of vector x.

4.3 Matrix Computations

Whereas the algorithms of the previous section were based on linearly connected systolic arrays, we now consider algorithms for two-dimensional systolic arrays. In Section 4.3.1 we show how two matrices can be multiplied on a hexagonally connected mesh of processors. Remarkably, this same systolic array with only minor modifications (Section 4.3.2) can be used to compute the LU-decomposition of a matrix. The building block of these systems is, as it was for the algorithms of Section 4.2, the inner-product-step processor. For these problems, however, the type (b) geometry for this processor shown in Figure 4–2 is appropriate.

4.3.1 Matrix Multiplication on a Hex-Connected Systolic Array

This section considers the problem of multiplying two n-by-n matrices. The matrix product $C = (c_{ij})$ of $A = (a_{ij})$ and $B = (b_{ij})$ can be computed by the following recurrences:

$$
\begin{aligned}
c_{ij}^{(1)} &= 0, \\
c_{ij}^{(k+1)} &= c_{ij}^{(k)} + a_{ik}b_{kj}, \\
c_{ij} &= c_{ij}^{(n+1)}.
\end{aligned}
\qquad (4\text{--}4)
$$

Let A and B be n-by-n band matrices with band widths w_A and w_B. These recurrences can be evaluated by pipelining the elements of A, B, and C through a systolic array which consists of $w_A w_B$ hex-connected inner-product-step processors. A systolic array that computes the matrix product

$$\begin{bmatrix} a_{11} & a_{12} & & & \\ a_{21} & a_{22} & a_{23} & & \text{0} \\ a_{31} & a_{32} & a_{33} & a_{34} & \\ & & a_{42} & & \cdot \\ \text{0} & & & \cdot & \cdot \end{bmatrix} \begin{bmatrix} b_{11} & b_{12} & b_{13} & & \\ b_{21} & b_{22} & b_{23} & b_{24} & \text{0} \\ & b_{32} & b_{33} & b_{34} & b_{35} \\ & & b_{43} & & \cdot \\ \text{0} & & & \cdot & \cdot \end{bmatrix} = \begin{bmatrix} c_{11} & c_{12} & c_{13} & c_{14} & \\ c_{21} & c_{22} & c_{23} & c_{24} & \text{0} \\ c_{31} & c_{32} & c_{33} & c_{34} & \\ c_{41} & c_{42} & & & \cdot \\ \text{0} & & & & \cdot \end{bmatrix} \qquad (4\text{-}5)$$

$$\qquad\qquad A \qquad\qquad\qquad\qquad B \qquad\qquad\qquad\qquad C$$

is shown in Figure 4–11. The elements in the bands of A, B, and C move through the systolic network in three different directions. Each c_{ij} is initialized to zero as it enters the network through the bottom boundaries. (For the more general problem of computing $AB + D$ where $D = (d_{ij})$ is another band matrix, each c_{ij} should be initialized as d_{ij}.) Each c_{ij} is able to accumulate all its terms before it leaves the network through the upper boundaries. Figure 4–12 shows four steps in the operation of this hexagonally connected systolic array. The data flow of this systolic array can be studied more closely by making transparencies of the band matrices shown in the figures, and moving them over the network picture as described.

The multiplication of two n-by-n band matrices A and B whose band widths are w_A and w_B can be performed in only $3n + \min(w_A, w_B)$ time on $w_A w_B$ hex-connected processors. In any row or column of the network, only one out of every three processors is active at any given time. Therefore, it is possible to use about $w_A w_B / 3$ processors by coalescing adjacent processors.

Another way of making use of the processors on the off-beats is to multiplex the systolic array as was mentioned in Section 2.2. Having several problem instances to solve at one time is a situation that arises when a large problem instance can be broken down into smaller instances which fit the size of the hardware. Matrix multiplication can be decomposed by using the distributive law to express each of the large n-by-n matrices as the sum of smaller band matrices which fit on the

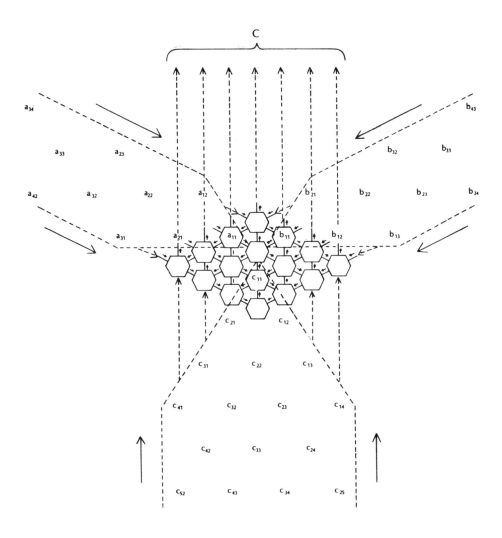

Figure 4–11: A hex-connected systolic array that computes the matrix product shown in Equation (4–5).

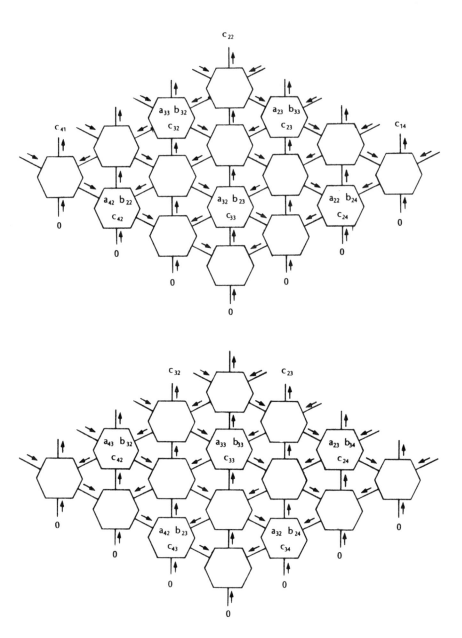

Figure 4–12: The operation of the hex-connected systolic array in Figure 4–11.

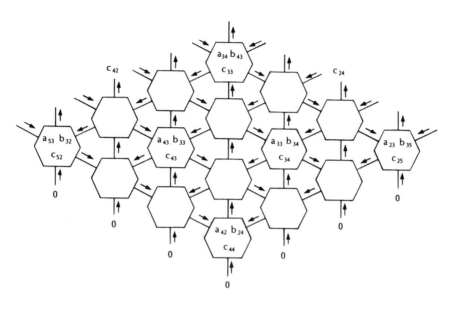

hardware. This decomposition also points up an advantage of the systolic system for matrix multiplication proposed here. If the host computer system can block transfer the elements of the matrices to the systolic device, problem instances of size nw_Aw_B can be handled by a systolic array of w_Aw_B processors without interrupting the host. A hardware design which required all data to be loaded into the device, on the other hand, could only cope with problems of size w_Aw_B before interrupting the host.

4.3.2 *LU*-Decomposition on a Hex-Connected Systolic Array

The problem of factoring a matrix A into lower and upper triangular matrices L and U is called *LU-decomposition*. The following equation shows the factorization when A is a band matrix with $p = 4$ and $q = 4$.

$$
\begin{bmatrix}
a_{11} & a_{12} & a_{13} & a_{14} & & & & 0 \\
a_{21} & a_{22} & a_{23} & a_{24} & a_{25} & & & \\
a_{31} & a_{32} & a_{33} & a_{34} & a_{35} & & & \\
a_{41} & a_{42} & a_{43} & & & & & \\
& a_{52} & a_{53} & & & & & \\
0 & & & & & & & \ddots
\end{bmatrix}
=
\begin{bmatrix}
1 & & & & & & \\
l_{21} & 1 & & & & 0 & \\
l_{31} & l_{32} & 1 & & & & \\
l_{41} & l_{42} & l_{43} & 1 & & & \\
& l_{52} & l_{53} & & & & \\
0 & & & & & & \ddots
\end{bmatrix}
\begin{bmatrix}
u_{11} & u_{12} & u_{13} & u_{14} & & 0 \\
& u_{22} & u_{23} & u_{24} & u_{25} & \\
& & u_{33} & u_{34} & u_{35} & \\
& & & & & \\
0 & & & & & \ddots
\end{bmatrix}
\tag{4-6}
$$

$$\qquad\qquad A \qquad\qquad\qquad\qquad L \qquad\qquad\qquad\qquad U$$

Once the L and U factors are known, it is relatively easy to invert A or solve the linear system $Ax = b$. (We dealt with the latter problem in Section 4.2.2.) This section describes a hex-connected systolic array for computing LU-decompositions.

The systolic algorithm proposed here assumes that the LU-decomposition can be performed without pivoting, which is true, for example, when A is a symmetric positive-definite, or an irreducible, diagonally dominant matrix. The triangular matrices $L = (l_{ij})$ and $U = (u_{ij})$ can then be evaluated according to the following recurrences:

$$a_{ij}^{(1)} = a_{ij},$$

$$a_{ij}^{'(k+1)} = a_{ij}^{(k)} + l_{ik}(-u_{kj}),$$

$$l_{ik} = \begin{cases} 0 & \text{if } i < k, \\ 1 & \text{if } i = k, \\ a_{ik}^{(k)}/u_{kk} & \text{if } i > k, \end{cases}$$

$$u_{kj} = \begin{cases} 0 & \text{if } k > j, \\ a_{kj}^{(k)} & \text{if } k \le j. \end{cases}$$

The evaluation of these recurrences can be pipelined on a systolic array of hex-connected processors. A global view of this pipelined computation is shown in Figure 4–13 for the LU-decomposition problem from Equation (4–6). The systolic array in Figure 4–13 is constructed as follows. All processors except for those on the upper boundaries are inner-product-step processors which form exactly the matrix multiplication network presented in Section 4.3.1. Of the processors on the upper boundary, the one denoted by a circle is a division processor like the one from Section 4.2.2. It forwards its input upward unchanged, but also computes the reciprocal and outputs this down to the left. The other processors on the upper boundaries are again inner-product-step processors, but their orientation is changed: the ones on the upper left boundary are rotated 120 degrees clockwise; the ones on the upper right boundary are rotated 120 degrees counterclockwise.

The flow of data on the systolic array is indicated by arrows in the figure. As in the hexagonal systolic array for matrix multiplication, each processor operates on real data only once every three clock ticks. Figure 4–14 illustrates four steps in the operation of the systolic array. Notice that since A is a band matrix with $p = 4$ and $q = 4$, when a_{52} enters the network, for example, it can be viewed as $a_{52}^{(2)}$. In general for this network, $a_{i+3,\,i}^{(k)} = a_{i+3,\,i}$ and $a_{i,\,i+3}^{(k)} = a_{i,\,i+3}$, where $1 \le k \le i$ and $i \ge 2$.

There are several equivalent systolic arrays that reflect only minor changes to the network presented in this section. For example, the elements of L and U can be

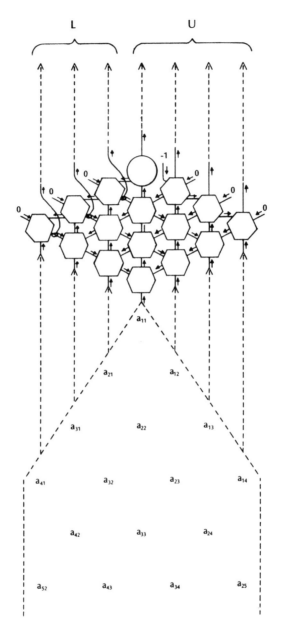

Figure 4–13: The hex-connected systolic array for pipelining the LU-decomposition
of the band matrix in Equation (4–6).

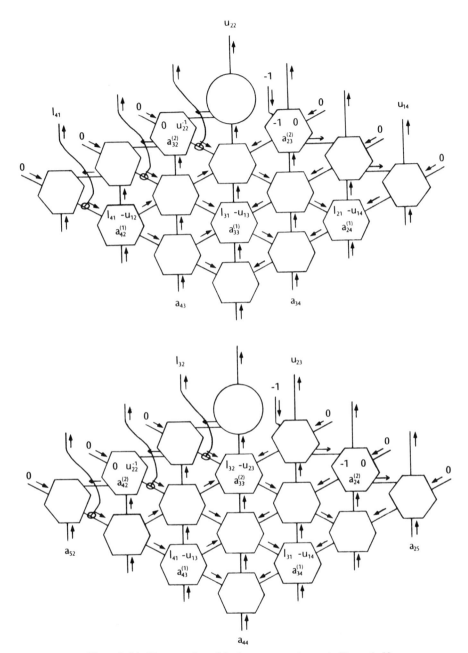

Figure 4–14: The operation of the hex-connected array in Figure 4–13.

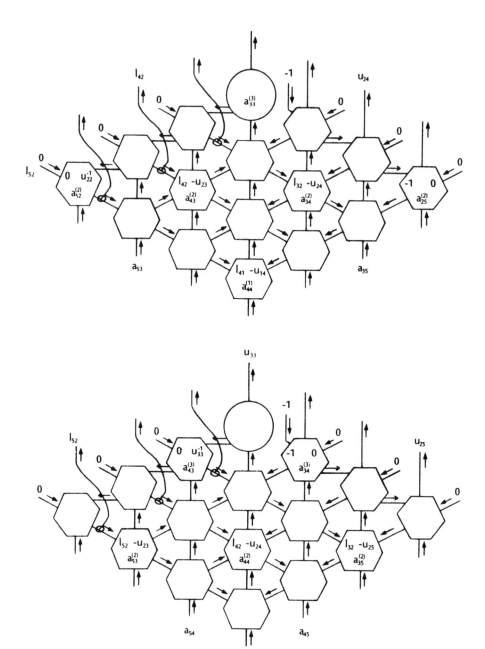

retrieved as output in a number of different ways. Also, the -1 input to the network can be changed to a $+1$ if the special processor at the top of the network computes minus the reciprocal of its input. The techniques used in previous sections to augment the processor utilization can of course be used.

If A is an n-by-n band matrix with band width $w = p+q-1$, a systolic array having no more than pq hex-connected processors can compute the LU-decomposition of A in time $3n + \min(p, q)$. If A is an n-by-n dense matrix, then n^2 hex-connected processors can compute the L and U matrices in $4n$ clock ticks. It is not to be forgotten that these complexities include I/O, control, and data movement.

Since the matrix multiplication systolic array forms the largest part of the LU-decomposition systolic array, both algorithms could easily be embodied in the same physical device. Recall also that the systolic array that multiplied matrices with vectors (Section 4.2.1) and the systolic array that solved triangular linear systems (Section 4.2.2) could easily be built as the same device. This is due to the similarity of the defining recurrences and the fact that the problems are in a sense inverses.

PART II

AREA-EFFICIENT LAYOUTS

CHAPTER 5

Preliminaries

5.1 Introduction

The systolic algorithms investigated in Part I were based primarily on array and tree interconnection schemes. That arrays can be embedded in the plane using little area should come as no surprise. But how much area does a tree require? The next few chapters will examine the problem in an abstract setting: *"Given a graph, produce an area-efficient layout."*

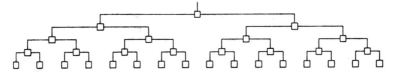

Figure 5-1: An $O(n \lg n)$ layout of a complete binary tree.

To illustrate the subtleties inherent in this problem, consider the problem of laying out a complete binary tree of $n = 2^k - 1$ vertices. Figure 5-1 shows an obvious solution that requires $O(n \lg n)$ area—$O(n)$ across the bottom times $O(\lg n)$ height. Observe that as we ascend the tree from the leaves to the root, the number of wires is halved from one level to the next, but the length of the wires doubles. This means that the amount of wire devoted to each level of the tree is the same. The recurrence that describes the area required by this layout is $A(n) = 1$ for $n = 1$, and

$$A(n) = 2A(\lfloor n/2 \rfloor) + n/2$$

for $n = 2^k - 1$ where $k > 1$.

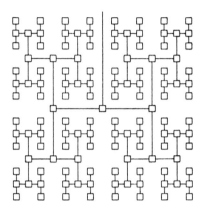

Figure 5-2: The H-tree layout of a complete binary tree.

There is a more efficient solution to this embedding problem. The so-called *H-tree* layout [29] shown in Figure 5-2 requires only $O(n)$ area in spite of the fact that relatively long wires are used towards the root of the tree. In this layout the number of wires is halved from level to level as we ascend to the root, but the length of the wires doubles only every two levels. Whereas the standard $O(n \lg n)$ layout uses just one dimension for routing most of the wires, the H-tree makes better use of both spatial dimensions. The recurrence describing the area required by the H-tree is more complex than the previous one because of its nonlinear form: $A(n) = 1$ for $n = 1$, and

$$A(n) = 4A(\lfloor n/4 \rfloor) + 4\sqrt{A(\lfloor n/4 \rfloor)} + 1$$

for $n = 2 \cdot 4^k - 1$ where $k \geq 1$.

This recurrence can be solved by taking the square root of both sides of the equation and rewriting it in terms of $\sqrt{A(n)}$, the length of the edge of the layout. The new recurrence is a simple divide-and-conquer recurrence, which has solution $O(\sqrt{n})$ for the edge of the layout.

The remainder of this chapter contains background material which will be used in later chapters. Section 5.2 contains a formulation of the VLSI layout model, and Section 5.3 gives the definition of a separator theorem. In Section 5.4 a nonlinear recurrence equation is solved which describes the area of layouts generated by the layout algorithm of Chapter 6.

5.2 The VLSI Model for Layouts

Before presenting a model for layouts, it is worthwhile to examine some of the attributes of VLSI technologies. VLSI components—wires and transistors—are constrained to lie in layers on a wafer of silicon. Because the number of layers is small (usually under six), the size of a VLSI chip can be measured by the total area of silicon used—the layers contributing to the ability of wires to cross. Every VLSI fabrication process has a natural metric, the *minimum feature size* λ, which is the width of the narrowest wire that can be manufactured.[9] The smallest transistor that can be manufactured is a square with edge λ and area λ^2. Since a wire of length L consumes λL area, it is not unusual for much of the area of a chip to be consumed by wires.

Intuitively, the VLSI model should make one-to-one correspondences between edges in the graph and data paths in the layout, and between vertices in the graph and processors in the layout. The mapping between edges and data paths seems straightforward enough, but there are issues to be resolved in establishing a correspondence between vertices and processors. One problem is that a vertex in a graph may have large degree, and yet on an integrated circuit, an arbitrarily large number of wires cannot come together at a single point. There just isn't enough room. A second problem arises from the fact that a processor must occupy nonzero area. What assumptions should be made about the size and shape of that area?

---

[9]Mead and Conway [28] in fact define λ to be half the width of the narrowest manufacturable wire.

We resolve these difficulties by restricting the discussion to classes of graphs with vertex degrees that are bounded by a constant, and by further assuming that vertices require only a constant area of silicon. This assumption is similar to the one made in Section 1.4 which helped ensure that combinational logic settled quickly. The results of this part, however, can apply to more complex models than the systolic model. For example, there is a simple transformation from an arbitrary graph to a trivalent graph such that each vertex of the original graph is a block of the trivalent graph. If processors in an alternative model can be decomposed in this way, the results will apply. In another variant of the model several processors may be connected by a single data path. By considering bipartite graphs—vertices in one set represent processors and those in the other represent data paths—many of the same results hold.

Having resolved the graph-theoretic issues, we now turn to the modeling of the layouts themselves. The VLSI model proposed here is similar to that of Thompson [41] in which wires have unit width and only a constant number (two) may cross at a point. Vertices are placed on a rectangular grid so that each lies within a grid square. Edges run horizontally and vertically, one per grid square, except that an edge running horizontally may cross one running vertically.[10]

Layouts that are designed with this model have the property that they are *sliceable.* That is, a horizontal or vertical line can be used to bisect the layout, the pieces can be moved apart, and the severed wires can be reconnected to realize the original topology. Slicing can be used to generate new layouts from old ones. For example, Figure 5-3 shows how slicing enables a new edge to be routed between two existing vertices in a layout. Two horizontal and two vertical cuts are made through the layout to expose the the vertices that are to be connected. (Actually,

---

[10]So that wires do not change often from one layer to another, many wire-routing programs use a *Manhattan* scheme [22] in which all horizontally running wires are placed on one layer and all vertically running wires on another.

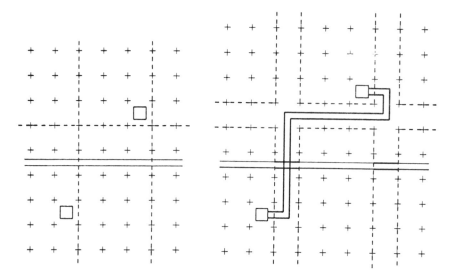

Figure 5-3: Two horizontal and two vertical slices
are more than sufficient to route an edge.

two slices in one direction and one in the other always suffice.) The pieces are separated by a grid unit, the severed edges are reconnected across the gaps, and a new edge that connects the vertices is run through the gaps. If the length in grid units of the original layout was L and the width W, the new layout has length at most $L+2$ and width at most $W+2$. It should be noticed that the slices through the layout must be straight—a staircase cut may require the pieces to be separated by more than a single grid unit for a new edge to be routed.

5.3 Separator Theorems

Lipton and Tarjan [25] showed that any planar graph of n vertices can be divided into two subgraphs of approximately the same size by removing only $O(\sqrt{n})$ vertices. Since the subgraphs are themselves planar, this *separator theorem* provides a basis for exploiting the divide-and-conquer paradigm [1]. We shall find it convenient to alter the definition of separator theorem that Lipton and Tarjan give. Whereas they bisect a graph by removing vertices, we shall remove edges. Since we are principally concerned with classes of graphs with bounded degree, the definition we give is equivalent except for the values of the constants in the definition.

Definition: Let S be a class of graphs closed under the subgraph relation, that is, if G is an element of S, and G' is a subgraph of G, then G' is also an element of S. An $f(n)$-*separator theorem* for S is a theorem of the following form.

There exist constants α_S and c_S where $0 < \alpha_S \leq 1/2$ and $c_S > 0$ such that if G is an n-vertex graph in S, then by removing at most $c_S f(n)$ edges, G can be partitioned into disjoint subgraphs G_1 and G_2 having αn and $(1-\alpha)n$ vertices respectively, where $\alpha_S \leq \alpha \leq 1-\alpha_S$.[11]

The set of removed edges is called the *cut set* of the bisection, and $f(n)$ is called the *width* of the bisection.

This definition is adequate for Lipton and Tarjan's $\sqrt{n}$-separator theorem because the class of planar graphs is closed under the subgraph relation. But there are many classes of graphs for which the same divide-and-conquer approach works, yet the class is not closed under the subgraph relation. The notion of separability can be extended by taking the closure of the original class of graphs with the subgraphs postulated by the separator theorem. Using this interpretation of separability, it is easy to show [24] that the class of trees has a 1-separator theorem. (The class of trees is not closed under the subgraph relation, although the class of *forests* of trees is.) We shall give additional separator theorems in Section 6.4.

---

[11] Throughout this paper it is assumed without loss of generality that α is chosen to permit αn to be an integer. This assumption is preferred over the use of floor or ceiling functions because it will be useful to identify the particular values of α and because it makes the mathematical formulae more readable.

5.4 A Nonlinear Recurrence

Suppose S is a class of graphs for which an $f(n)$-separator theorem has been proved. In Chapter 6 we shall show how to lay out any graph in S. In this section we investigate a nonlinear recurrence equation that will be used to relate $f(n)$ to the area of the layout.

Let $A(1)$ be a positive constant, and let $A(n)$ be defined on any integer $n \geq 2$ by

$$A(n) = \max_{\alpha_S \leq \alpha \leq 1-\alpha_S} (\sqrt{A(\alpha n) + A((1-\alpha)n)} + f(n))^2, \qquad (5\text{--}1)$$

for some $0 < \alpha_S \leq 1/2$.

Given a particular $f(n)$, there are standard methods for solving such a recurrence. We shall use a technique, however, that will enable us to solve this recurrence for broad classes of $f(n)$. We shall define a simpler function $B(n)$, which will be shown to have the property

$$A(n) \leq nB^2(n) \qquad (5\text{--}2)$$

for all n. By providing an upper bound for $B(n)$, it will be easy to use (5–2) to bound $A(n)$.

We define $B(n)$ as $\sqrt{A(1)}$ for $n = 1$, and as

$$B(n) = \max_{\alpha_S \leq \alpha \leq 1-\alpha_S} (B(\alpha n) + f(n)/\sqrt{n})$$

for $n > 1$. Property (5–2) holds for $n = 1$ by the definition of $B(1)$. Making the inductive assumption that it holds for values less than n,

$$A(n) \leq \max_{\alpha_s \leq \alpha \leq 1-\alpha_s} \left(\sqrt{\alpha n B^2(\alpha n) + (1-\alpha)n B^2((1-\alpha)n)} + f(n) \right)^2$$

$$\leq \max_{\alpha_s \leq \alpha \leq 1-\alpha_s} \left(\sqrt{\alpha n B^2(\alpha n) + (1-\alpha)n B^2(\alpha n)} + f(n) \right)^2 \qquad (5\text{-}3)$$

$$\leq \max_{\alpha_s \leq \alpha \leq 1-\alpha_s} \left(\sqrt{n B^2(\alpha n)} + f(n) \right)^2$$

$$\leq \max_{\alpha_s \leq \alpha \leq 1-\alpha_s} n \left(B(\alpha n) + f(n)/\sqrt{n} \right)^2$$

$$= n B^2(n).$$

Line (5-3) in this proof follows from the consideration of two cases. If $B(\alpha n) \geq B((1-\alpha)n)$ for the value of α that realizes the maximum, then (5-3) be derived from the previous line by straightforward substitution of $B(\alpha n)$ for $B((1-\alpha)n)$. On the other hand, if $B(\alpha n) < B((1-\alpha)n)$, then substitution of $B((1-\alpha)n)$ for $B(\alpha n)$ followed by a change of variable of $1-\alpha$ for α yields the same result.

It remains to evaluate $B(n)$ which, except for the maximization, is a simple divide-and-conquer recurrence that can be solved by iteration. Thus

$$B(n) = \frac{f(n)}{\sqrt{n}} + \frac{f(\alpha_1 n)}{\sqrt{\alpha_1 n}} + \frac{f(\alpha_1 \alpha_2 n)}{\sqrt{\alpha_1 \alpha_2 n}} + \ldots + B(\alpha_1 \alpha_2 \ldots \alpha_r n) \qquad (5\text{-}4)$$

where $r \leq -\log_{1-\alpha_s} n$; each value $\alpha_1, \alpha_2, \ldots, \alpha_r$ is the value of α that realizes the maximum at each stage of the iteration; and the product $\alpha_1 \alpha_2 \ldots \alpha_r$ equals $1/n$. Upper bounds for Equation (5-4) can be determined on the basis of suitable assumptions about $f(n)$. The upper bounds in Table 5-4 were determined by evaluating this summation according to the indicated assumptions about $f(n)$. The lower bounds for $A(n)$ were derived by defining a function $C(n)$ that is similar to $B(n)$ but that provides the bound $A(n) \geq n C^2(n)$.

To demonstrate the upper bound results for the third entry, it is insufficient to

Table 5-4: Solutions of Recurrence (5-1).

$f(n)$	$B(n)$	$A(n)$
$O(n^q)$, $q < 1/2$	$O(1)$	$\Theta(n)$
$\Theta(\sqrt{n}\,\lg^k n)$, $k \geq 0$	$O(\lg^{k+1} n)$	$\Theta(n\,\lg^{2k+2} n)$
$\Omega(n^q)$, $q > 1/2\dagger$	$O(f(n)/\sqrt{n})$	$\Theta(f^2(n))$

†See text for an explanation of this entry.

assume only that $f(n) = \Omega(n^q)$ for some $q > 1/2$ as the table implies. In addition the function $f(n)/\sqrt{n}$ must be well-behaved in the following sense.

Definition: A function $g(n)$ is said to satisfy *Regularity Condition C1* if there exist positive constants c_1 and β_1 such that $c_1 < 1$, $\beta_1 \leq 1/2$, and $g(\beta n) \leq c_1 g(n)$ for all sufficiently large n and all β in the range $\beta_1 \leq \beta \leq 1-\beta_1$.

Making the assumption that $f(n)/\sqrt{n}$ satisfies Condition C1 with $\beta_1 = \alpha_S$, we can now prove the third line of the table. For large n and $\alpha_S \leq \alpha_1 \leq 1-\alpha_S$, we have

$$\frac{f(\alpha_1 n)}{\sqrt{\alpha_1 n}} \leq c_1 \frac{f(n)}{\sqrt{n}},$$

and in general for each term in Equation (5-4)

$$\frac{f(\alpha_1\alpha_2\ldots\alpha_k n)}{\sqrt{\alpha_1\alpha_2\ldots\alpha_k n}} \leq c_1^k \frac{f(n)}{\sqrt{n}}.$$

Substituting these terms in Equation (5-4) gives the bound

$$B(n) \leq \frac{f(n)}{\sqrt{n}}\left(1 + c_1 + c_1^2 + \ldots\right) + constant,$$

which is $O(f(n)/\sqrt{n})$ since $c_1 < 1$. The constant arises from the finite number of values that are not sufficiently large according to the regularity condition.

We have just shown that the third entry in the table holds if $f(n)/\sqrt{n}$ satisfies Condition C1. What can be deduced from a weaker assumption? Suppose, for example, that we only assume that $f(n)/\sqrt{n}$ is monotonically nondecreasing, that is

$$\frac{f(\alpha n)}{\sqrt{\alpha n}} \leq \frac{f(n)}{\sqrt{n}},$$

for all $n \geq 2$ and all α in the range $\alpha_S \leq \alpha \leq 1-\alpha$. Since there are only $O(\lg n)$ terms in the summation (5-4), it follows that $B(n) = O((f(n)\lg n)/\sqrt{n})$ and $A(n) = O(f^2(n)\lg^2 n)$. A factor of $\lg^2 n$ in area is paid because monotonicity is a weaker constraint than Regularity Condition C1 on the well-behavedness of $f(n)/\sqrt{n}$.

The layout construction of the following section will need to assume that $A(n)$ is itself well-behaved according to a different regularity condition.

> **Definition:** A function $g(n)$ is said to satisfy *Regularity Condition C2* if there exist positive constants c_2 and β_2 such that $\beta_2 \leq 1/2$ and $g(\beta n) \geq c_2 g(n)$ for all $n \geq 2$ and for all β in the range $\beta_2 \leq \beta \leq 1-\beta_2$.

The qualification "for all $n \geq 2$" in this definition seems to be stronger than the phrase "for all sufficiently large n" which was used in the definition of Regularity Condition C1. If all the values of $g(n)$ are positive, however, the two qualifications are equivalent—although the values for the constants may be different.

Condition C2 is always satisfied by the solutions of $A(n)$ shown in the first two lines of Table 5-4, but not necessarily by that in the third line. To guarantee that $A(n)$ satisfies Condition C2 in this instance, it is sufficient to assume that $f(n)$ itself satisfies Condition C2 in addition to the previous assumption that $f(n)/\sqrt{n}$ satisfies C1.

The reader should be aware that most of the functions arising from a separator theorem will indeed satisfy these regularity conditions. As an example, the conditions are satisfied by all functions of the form $cn^q\lg^k n$ for constants c, q, and k

such that c and q are positive. Similar regularity conditions are assumed elsewhere in the literature (e.g. [1], [4], and [6]) in order to determine the asymptotic behavior of general complexity functions.

.

CHAPTER 6

A Layout Algorithm

6.1 Introduction

The main contribution of this chapter is an algorithm which, given a separator theorem for a class of graphs, can lay out any graph in the class. First, however, some results regarding the areas and *aspect ratios* of layouts are proved in Section 6.2. Section 6.3 presents the layout construction. Among the corollaries of this result are that an arbitrary binary tree with n vertices can be laid out in linear area, and planar graphs can be laid out in $O(n \lg^2 n)$ area. In Section 6.5 an implementation of the layout algorithm is presented which is based on the UNION-FIND algorithm analyzed by Tarjan [40], and it is shown that the time required for maintaining the representation of a layout is nearly linear.

6.2 Areas and Aspect Ratios

The size and shape of a rectangle are uniquely determined by its *length L* and its *width W*, where we shall assume that $L \geq W > 0$. But there is another coordinate space for specifying sizes and shapes of rectangles—*area* and *aspect ratio*. Everyone is familiar with area and knows that the area can be defined as the product $L W$. The aspect ratio σ is defined as the quantity W/L, which is at most one. Given the area and aspect ratio of a rectangle, its length and width are given by $L = \sqrt{A/\sigma}$ and $W = \sqrt{\sigma A}$.

Suppose a graph has a VLSI layout of area A and aspect ratio σ. It is natural to ask whether there are other layouts of the graph that have different dimensions but similar area. The following theorem shows that a long and skinny layout can be made into a square layout (aspect ratio of one) by paying only a constant factor increase in area.

> **Theorem 6-1:** If the bounding rectangle of a given layout has area A, then there exists a topologically equivalent layout that can be enclosed in a square whose area is at most $3A$.

Proof. Let the length and width of the original layout be integers L and W. If $L < 3W$, then a square with side L satisfies the constraints of the theorem. Now suppose $L \geq 3W$. The layout can be sliced in several places and "folded" like a roadmap with the severed wires connected around the corners. Figure 6-1 shows a square with side $s = \lfloor \sqrt{3A} \rfloor$ in which a rectangle has been folded. This rectangle is the longest rectangle of width W that can be folded into the square, so if we can prove that the length of this rectangle is at least L, then we will have demonstrated that the original layout can also be folded to fit in the square.

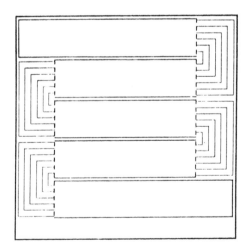

Figure 6-1: A layout can be "folded" to fit into a square.

Let $k = \lfloor s/W \rfloor$ be the number of pieces into which this longest rectangle of width W has been folded. The rectangle is made up of two long pieces and $k-2$ short pieces. Since $L \geq 3W$ implies $s \geq 3W$, the short pieces must be at least $s/3$ grid units long, and the long pieces must have length at least $2s/3$. Thus the total length of the folded rectangle is at least $(k-2)s/3 + 2(2s/3) = s(k+2)/3$.

Because k is the largest number of pieces of width W that can be folded into the square, it follows that $k+1$ pieces of width W will not fit. Therefore, the length s of the side of the square must be strictly less than $W(k+1)$, which means

$$s \leq W(k+1) - 1.$$

By definition of s, the quantity $(s+1)^2$ must be strictly larger than $3A$, and hence

$$3LW \leq (s+1)^2 - 1 = s(s+2).$$

Substituting for s,

$$
\begin{aligned}
3LW &\leq s(W(k+1) - 1 + 2) \\
&= s(W(k+1) + 1) \\
&\leq sW(k+2)
\end{aligned}
$$

since $W \geq 1$. Cancelling W from both sides and dividing by three yields $L \leq s(k+2)/3$. But the righthand side of this inequality is the value that we earlier demonstrated was less than or equal to the total length of the folded rectangle. Thus L is less than this total length, which was to be proved.[12] □

Can one "unfold" a square layout to make it arbitrarily long and skinny without paying a large increase in area? Not always, and a unit square layout provides the counterexample. If we insist that the side of the square be large, the answer is still no. For example, we showed in the introduction that an n-leaf complete binary tree can be laid out in $O(n)$ area. But in Section 7.2, we shall prove

---

[12]The worst case is achieved by a one-by-three rectangle. Larger rectangles with this aspect ratio do significantly better, however.

that the minimum dimension of that area must have order at least $\lg n$. Thus to achieve good upper bounds for layouts, it seems prudent to avoid those that have small aspect ratios.

The technique presented in Section 6.3 to construct area-efficient layouts recursively bisects rectangular areas. To avoid creating arbitrarily long and skinny rectangles during the recursion, it is important that the aspect ratios of the generated rectangles be bounded below by a positive constant. The next lemma sets forth conditions whereby a rectangle whose aspect ratio is so bounded can be bisected into two rectangles whose aspect ratios are similarly bounded.

> **Lemma 6-2:** Let R be a rectangle with area A and aspect ratio σ_R, where $\sigma_R \geq \sigma$ for some σ in the range $0 < \sigma \leq 1/2$. Suppose R is bisected parallel to its short side into two rectangles R_1 and R_2 whose areas A_1 and A_2 are ξA and $(1-\xi)A$ for some ξ in the range $\sigma \leq \xi \leq 1-\sigma$. Then the aspect ratios of the subrectangles are bounded below by σ, that is, $\sigma_{R_1} \geq \sigma$ and $\sigma_{R_2} \geq \sigma$.

Proof. Without loss of generality, we consider R_1 only. The proof may be broken into two cases. If $\xi \geq \sigma_R$, then the aspect ratio of R_1 is σ_R/ξ. This is bounded below by σ since $\sigma \leq \sigma_R$ implies that $\sigma < \sigma/\xi \leq \sigma_R/\xi$. On the other hand if $\xi < \sigma_R$, then the aspect ratio of R_1 is ξ/σ_R. But σ bounds ξ from below, and hence $\sigma < \sigma/\sigma_R \leq \xi/\sigma_R$. $\square$

Suppose a square is divided into two rectangles so that the ratio of the area of the smaller to the larger is at worst $\sigma/(1-\sigma)$, and then the rectangles are themselves subdivided by at worst the same ratio of areas, and so forth. Lemma 6-2 says that if the bisection is always parallel to the short side, then no rectangle is ever generated whose aspect ratio is worse than σ. The divide-and-conquer construction in Section 6.3 will use this result.

6.3 Area-Efficient Layout Construction

Area-efficient layouts can be obtained through the use of the divide-and-conquer paradigm. This section presents a construction which takes a graph and divides it into two subgraphs which are recursively embedded. The two sublayouts are then sliced to expose the vertices with edges in the cut set and then those edges are routed as described in Section 5.2.

> **Theorem 6-3:** Let S be a class of graphs for which an $f(n)$-separator theorem has been proved, and let α_S and c_S be the constants postulated by the separator theorem. Suppose $A(n)$, which is defined by $A(n) = 1/c_S^2$ for $n = 1$, and
>
> $$A(n) = \max_{\alpha_S \leq \alpha \leq 1-\alpha_S} \left(\sqrt{A(\alpha n) + A((1-\alpha)n)} + f(n) \right)^2 \qquad (6\text{-}1)$$
>
> for $n > 1$, satisfies Regularity Condition C2 with $\beta_2 = \alpha_S$. Then any n-vertex graph G in S can be embedded in any rectangle whose area is at least
>
> $$A_S(n) = (4c_S^2/\sigma_S) A(n), \qquad (6\text{-}2)$$
>
> and whose aspect ratio is at worst σ_S, where σ_S is defined to be the value of c_2 in the regularity condition.[13]

Proof. Let G be an n-vertex graph in S. The following recursive construction shows how to embed G in a rectangle R whose aspect ratio σ_R is at most σ_S and whose area is $A_S(n)$. Without loss of generality, view rectangle R so that the longer side which has length $\sqrt{A_S(n)/\sigma_R}$ is parallel to the horizontal axis, and so that the shorter side which has length $\sqrt{\sigma_R A_S(n)}$ is vertical.

Step 0. *Initial condition.* If $n = 1$ then the graph G is just a single vertex. Rectangle R, which has area $A_S(1)$, must contain a grid square because each

---

[13]Thus the entries for $A(n)$ in Table 5-4 can be used to evaluate $A_S(n)$ since these two functions differ by at most a constant factor.

dimension of R is at least two, a fact that is easily verified. Thus the theorem is true for the initial condition by simply embedding the single vertex in the grid square and returning this layout as the result of the construction.

Step 1. *Partition.* Using the $f(n)$-separator theorem, divide G into two disjoint subgraphs G_1 and G_2 that have $\alpha_G n$ and $(1 - \alpha_G)n$ vertices respectively, where $\alpha_S \leq \alpha_G \leq 1 - \alpha_S$. The number of edges in the cut set is at most $c_S f(n)$.

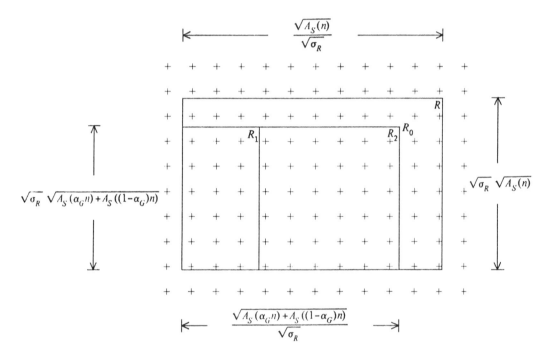

Figure 6-2: The relationships among rectangles in Step 2.

Step 2. *Solve the subproblems.* Remembering that rectangle R is oriented with its longer side horizontal, define R_0 to be a similar rectangle to R that has area $A_S(\alpha_G n) + A_S((1 - \alpha_G)n)$ and sits in the lower left corner of R. (See Figure 6-2.) Apply Lemma 6-2 with

$$\xi = \frac{A(\alpha_G n)}{A(\alpha_G n) + A((1 - \alpha_G)n)} = \frac{A_S(\alpha_G n)}{A_S(\alpha_G n) + A_S((1 - \alpha_G)n)}$$

to divide R_0 into two rectangles R_1 and R_2 whose areas are $A_S(\alpha_G n)$ and $A_S((1-\alpha_G)n)$. The aspect ratios of R_1 and R_2 are bounded below by σ_S since

$$\sigma_S \leq \frac{A(\alpha_G n)}{A(n)} \leq \frac{A(\alpha_G n)}{A(\alpha_G n) + A((1-\alpha_G)n)}$$

$$= 1 - \frac{A((1-\alpha_G)n)}{A(\alpha_G n) + A((1-\alpha_G)n)} \leq 1 - \frac{A((1-\alpha_G)n)}{A(n)} \leq 1 - \sigma_S,$$

which follows from the definition (6–1) of $A(n)$ and Regularity Condition C2. Now solve the subproblems by recursively embedding G_1 in R_1 and G_2 in R_2.

Step 3. *Marry the subproblems.* For each of the $c_S f(n)$ edges in the set of removed edges, make at most two horizontal and two vertical slices through R_0 to route the edge between its incident vertices as was shown in Figure 5–3. The length of this new layout is $length(R_0) + 2c_S f(n)$ and its width is $width(R_0) + 2c_S f(n)$. It remains to be shown that this layout actually fits in rectangle R, viz.

$$length(R) \geq length(R_0) + 2c_S f(n), \qquad (6\text{–}3)$$

$$width(R) \geq width(R_0) + 2c_S f(n). \qquad (6\text{–}4)$$

To prove these inequalities, mathematical induction can be used to give an alternative definition of $A_S(n)$ to that of Equation (6–2): $A_S(n) = 4/\sigma_S$ for $n = 1$, and

$$A_S(n) = \max_{\alpha_S \leq \alpha \leq 1 - \alpha_S} (\sqrt{A_S(\alpha n) + A_S((1-\alpha)n)} + 2c_S f(n)/\sqrt{\sigma_S})^2$$

for $n > 1$. We can now use this definition to prove Inequality (6–3) since

$$length(R) = \sqrt{A_S(n)/\sigma_R}$$

$$\geq \sqrt{(A_S(\alpha_G n) + A_S((1-\alpha_G)n))/\sigma_R} + 2c_S f(n)/\sqrt{\sigma_S \sigma_R}$$

$$\geq length(R_0) + 2c_S f(n),$$

which follows from the fact that $\sigma_S \sigma_R \leq 1$. The proof of Inequality (6–4) makes use of the fact that $\sigma_S \leq \sigma_R$, whence

$$
\begin{aligned}
width(R) &= \sqrt{\sigma_R A_S(n)} \\
&\geq \sqrt{\sigma_R}\,\left(\sqrt{A_S(\alpha_G n)+A_S((1-\alpha_G)n)} \,+\, 2\,c_S f(n)/\sqrt{\sigma_S}\right) \\
&\geq width(R_0) + 2\,c_S f(n)\sqrt{\sigma_R/\sigma_S} \\
&\geq width(R_0) + 2\,c_S f(n).
\end{aligned}
$$

We have shown that the layout actually fits within the bounds of rectangle R, which completes the proof of Theorem 6-3. $\square$

6.4 Corollaries of the Main Result[14]

Upper bounds on the areas of VLSI layouts for many graphs can be immediately derived as consequences Theorem 6-3 and Table 5-4. Some of these corollaries are enumerated in Table 6-3.

The separator theorems of Section 5.3 produce the first two results of the table. Since the class of tree graphs has a 1-separator theorem, the first line of Table 5-4 says that any tree or forest of trees has a layout whose area is linear in the number of vertices. Lipton and Tarjan's $\sqrt{n}$-separator theorem for planar graphs gives, according to Line 2 of Table 5-4, an $O(n\lg^2 n)$ area upper bound for the layout of any planar graph of n vertices.

Outerplanar graphs are triangulations of polygons, perhaps with some edges removed. The author has proved a 1-separator theorem for the class of outerplanar graphs, and thus these graphs have linear area layouts. The separator theorem for trees is subsumed by this result because every tree is an outerplanar graph.

The X-tree graph [34], which is shown in Figure 6-4, is a complete binary tree with brother connections. One could attempt to lay out this graph by modifying the

---

[14] The results reported in this section on trees and planar graphs have been discovered independently by L. G. Valiant [42]. In fact, Valiant was able to show that trees could be laid out in linear area with no crossovers. Also, R. W. Floyd and J. D. Ullman [11] have used similar techniques to show that any regular expression can be recognized by a linear-area circuit.

Table 6-3: Areas of graphs.

Class of graphs	Area of layout
Trees†	$O(n)$
Planar graphs	$O(n \lg^2 n)$
Outerplanar graphs†	$O(n)$
X-trees $(n = 2^k)$†	$O(n)$
k-dimensional meshes $(k > 2)$†	$O(n^{2-2/k})$
Graphs of genus k $(k > 0)$	$O(k^2 n \lg^2 n)$
Shuffle-exchange $(n = 2^{2^k})$	$O(n^2/\lg n)$
Cube-connected-cycles $(n = k2^k)$†	$O(n^2/\lg^2 n)$

†These results are optimal to within a constant factor.

H-tree layout (an interesting exercise), but proving that the class of X-trees has a $\lg n$-separator theorem is easier. Bisect the graph with a vertical line that cuts at most $(\lg n) + 1$ edges. Each of the two halves can be bisected similarly, once again cutting at most $(\lg n) + 1$ edges, where n is now the number of vertices in the half. Since $\lg n = O(n^q)$ for any positive q, Line 1 of Table 5-4 shows that any X-tree can be laid out in linear area.

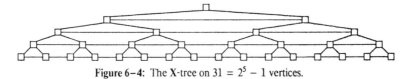

Figure 6-4: The X-tree on $31 = 2^5 - 1$ vertices.

A k-dimensional mesh is a graph in which each vertex is connected to its nearest neighbor in each of k dimensions. Any class of k-dimensional meshes for some constant k has an easily proved $n^{1-1/k}$-separator theorem, and thus if $k \geq 3$, an n-vertex graph in the class has an $O(n^{2-2/k})$ area layout by virtue of Line 3 of Table 5-4.

A graph of genus k is a graph that can be drawn with no crossovers on a sphere that has k handles attached. It has been shown [2] that there is a subset of $O(k\sqrt{n})$ vertices whose removal yields a planar graph. Applying Lipton and Tarjan's result gives a $k\sqrt{n}$-separator theorem. Line 2 of Table 5–4 provides an upper bound of $O(k^2 n \lg^2 n)$ for the layout area of an n-vertex graph of genus k.

In [17] Hoey and this author prove a separator theorem for the shuffle-exchange graph [37] on $n = 2^{2^k}$ vertices. Although the function in this separator theorem does not satisfy the regularity conditions of Section 5.4, the techniques of this paper do apply, and a $O(n^2/\lg n)$ area layout can be obtained which improves the bound of $O(n^2/\sqrt{n})$ given by Thompson [41]. Recently, however, we have been able to improve this result by showing that the $O(n^2/\lg n)$ bound holds for all shuffle-exchange graphs on $n = 2^k$ vertices. This new result, however, does not use the techniques in this paper.[15]

Preparata and Vuillemin provide an $O(n^2/\lg^2 n)$ area VLSI layout for their cube-connected-cycles network [33] on $n = k2^k$ vertices. The topology of this network, which is depicted in Figure 6–5, can be derived from a boolean hypercube of 2^k vertices by replacing each vertex with a cycle of k vertices. This graph has a $n/\lg n$-separator theorem since removing all edges in one dimension of the original hypercube bisects the graph, removal of those in another bisects the halves, and so forth for all k dimensions. The area bound $O(n^2/\lg^2 n)$ that is given by Line 3 of Table 5–4 is the same as the area of the layout which is given in [33].

Upper bounds in Table 6–3 that are optimal to within a constant factor are so designated in the table. The linear upper bounds are clearly optimal because every graph requires $\Omega(n)$ area. The other lower bounds can be obtained from a result of Thompson [41]. The *minimum bisection width* of a graph is defined to be the

---

[15]Recently, this result was improved to the optimal $O(n^2/\lg^2 n)$ by Kleitman, Leighton, Lepley, and Miller of MIT.

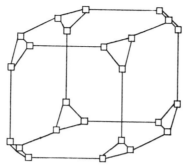

Figure 6-5: The cube-connected-cycles network on $24 = 3 \cdot 2^3$ vertices.

minimum number of edges that must be cut to divide the graph into a $\lfloor n/2 \rfloor$-vertex graph and a $\lceil n/2 \rceil$-vertex graph. Thompson proves that the area of a graph has order at least the square of the minimum bisection width of the graph. This lower bound argument is surprisingly similar to an analysis of printed circuit boards given in [39].

Using another of Thompson's arguments, it can be shown that the shuffle-exchange graph and the cube-connected-cycles graph have minimum bisection widths of order at least $n/\lg n$. This arises from the fact that these networks can realize an arbitrary permutation in $O(\lg n)$ communication steps. Thus if one of these graphs is partitioned into two halves, it must be possible to swap data items between the halves in $O(\lg n)$ time. Since there are $\Omega(n)$ data items to be swapped, at least order $n/\lg n$ data cross between the halves during each time unit, and hence the minimum bisection width of these graphs is $\Omega(n/\lg n)$. The area of any VLSI layout for these graphs must therefore have order at least $n^2/\lg^2 n$. Thus the upper bound for the cube-connected-cycles graph is optimal, but there is a discrepancy in the bounds for the shuffle-exchange graph.

There is also a discrepancy in the the upper and lower bounds for planar graphs. The methods given above give only a linear area lower bound compared with the $O(n \lg^2 n)$ upper bound. The author believes it more likely that the upper bound can be improved because he knows of no planar graph that requires more than linear area, and in addition, planar graphs appear to have considerably more structure than is captured by the $\sqrt{n}$-separator theorem alone.

6.5 An Efficient Implementation of the Layout Algorithm

If a separator theorem can be proved for a class of graphs, Theorem 6–3 can be used to give an upper bound on the area of a VLSI layout for a graph in the class. If, however, a *separator algorithm* is given for the class of graphs, the steps in the proof of Theorem 6–3 constitute an algorithm that can construct a VLSI layout for a graph in the class. In this section, we provide an efficient implementation of this algorithm and analyze its performance.

The layout algorithm uses the separator algorithm as a subroutine, and therefore has an execution time that depends upon the efficiencies of both this subroutine and the bookkeeping necessary for the production of a layout. The analysis here reflects this dichotomy. The total time required to lay out a graph of n vertices can be expressed as the sum of (i) the total time devoted to the repeated executions of the separator subroutine on the generated subgraphs plus (ii) the time devoted to the management of the layout representation. Later in this section, we shall present a fast bookkeeping scheme that is based on the UNION-FIND algorithm analyzed by Tarjan [40]. But first, we analyze the amount of time required by the many executions of the separator subroutine.

The layout procedure has no direct control over the efficiency of the separator subroutine. In fact, it might be the case that all the graph bisections have been previously computed so that the subroutine is deceptively fast. For the analysis here, however, we assume that the subroutine is invoked in-line, and that $s(n)$ is the time required by the separator subroutine to bisect a graph of n vertices. We can express the relationship of $S(n)$, the total amount of time required for all executions of the subroutine during the laying out of a graph of n vertices, to $s(n)$ by the recurrence $S(n) = 1$ for $n = 1$, and

$$S(n) \;=\; S(\alpha n) + S((1-\alpha)n) + s(n) \tag{6-5}$$

for $n > 1$, where α varies in the range $\alpha_S \leq \alpha \leq 1 - \alpha_S$.

Bounds for $S(n)$ can be determined by the same technique used to solve Recurrence (5-1). Define $R(n) = S(1)$ for $n = 1$, and

$$R(n) \;=\; \max_{\alpha_S \leq \alpha \leq 1-\alpha_S} R(\alpha n) + s(n)/n$$

for $n > 1$. The bound

$$S(n) \leq n\,R(n),$$

which holds for the case $n = 1$, also holds for all values of n greater than one, as is shown by induction:

$$
\begin{aligned}
S(n) \;&\leq\; \alpha n R(\alpha n) + (1-\alpha)n R((1-\alpha)n) + s(n) \\[4pt]
&\leq\; \max_{\alpha_S \leq \alpha \leq 1-\alpha_S} \alpha n R(\alpha n) + (1-\alpha)n R((1-\alpha)n) + s(n) \\[4pt]
&\leq\; \max_{\alpha_S \leq \alpha \leq 1-\alpha_S} n R(\alpha n) + s(n) \\[4pt]
&\leq\; n\,R(n).
\end{aligned}
$$

The results enumerated in Table 6-6 are derived by evaluating $R(n)$ to provide an upper bound on $S(n)$, and using a similar function to bound $S(n)$ from below. Let us look at this table in greater detail.

The first line is a bit of a red herring. It says that if the execution time of the separator subroutine is polynomially less than linear in the number of vertices in the graph, then the contribution to the total running time is linear. It should be apparent, however, that this precondition is rarely satisfied in practice. After all, it takes the subroutine at least linear time just to look at all of its input.

The second line of Table 6-6 is more usual—the subroutine requires approximately linear time. In this case, the total time required by all executions of the subroutine is only a logarithmic factor larger than the time needed by the initial

Table 6-6: Time devoted to the separator subroutine.

$s(n)$	$S(n)$
$O(n^q), \; q < 1$	$\Theta(n)$
$\Theta(n \lg^k n), \; k \geq 0$	$\Theta(n \lg^{k+1} n)$
$\Omega(n^q), \; q > 1\dagger$	$\Theta(s(n))$

†The function $s(n)/n$ must also satisfy Regularity Condition C1.

invocation of the separator subroutine on the graph presented as input to the layout procedure. Tree graphs have a linear-time 1-separator algorithm that is not difficult to construct, and thus according to the table, the layout algorithm would spend a total of $\Theta(n \lg n)$ time executing this as a subroutine when producing a layout for an n-vertex tree. Lipton and Tarjan's $\sqrt{n}$-separator algorithm for planar graphs also runs in linear time, and thus only $\Theta(n \lg n)$ time is needed for all of its executions.

The third line of the table says that if the execution time of the separator subroutine is polynomially greater than linear, then the time required by the first call, which bisects the n-vertex input graph, dominates the time for subsequent invocations. This analysis is based on the supposition that $s(n)/n$ satisfies Regularity Condition C1. When only monotonicity is assumed, the total time is $O(s(n) \lg n)$.

Now that the costs due to the $f(n)$-separator algorithm have been determined, we turn our attention to the bookkeeping required to maintain the layout representation. The implementation proposed here makes extensive use of the UNION-FIND algorithm analyzed by Tarjan [40]. This algorithm provides two instructions for the manipulation of disjoint sets. FIND(x) determines the name of the unique set containing element x, and UNION(X,Y,Z) combines the elements of sets X and Y into a new set Z. The analysis in [40] shows that the time required to execute n

UNION operations intermixed with $m > n$ FIND's is $O(ma(m, n))$ where $a(m, n)$ is related to a functional inverse of Ackermann's function and grows *extremely* slowly.[16] We do not go into a description of the algorithm here—a good one can be found in [1]—but we shall use the UNION and FIND operations and the results of Tarjan's analysis.

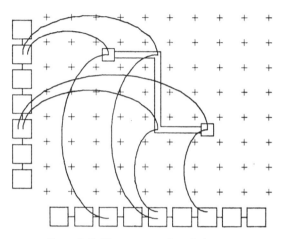

Figure 6–7: The representation of a layout.

The key to the performance of the layout procedure is the sparse representation of layouts depicted in Figure 6–7. Each important point of the layout is kept in two sets, an *x-set* that represents its x-coordinate in the layout, and a *y-set* that represents its y-coordinate. The important points in the layout are the vertices in the graph and the endpoints of the horizontal and vertical edge segments. The UNION-FIND data structure maintains the relationship between a point and its corresponding x- and y-sets. In Figure 6–7, this association is denoted by the curved arcs. All the x- and y-sets for a layout are kept in linked lists. The actual x-coordinate represented by a given x-set is therefore determined by its distance from the head of the list. Pointers are used to maintain relationships between

---

[16]Tarjan comments that for all practical purposes, $a(n, n)$ is less than or equal to three.

points.   For example, an edge segment is represented by a pointer from one
endpoint to the other.

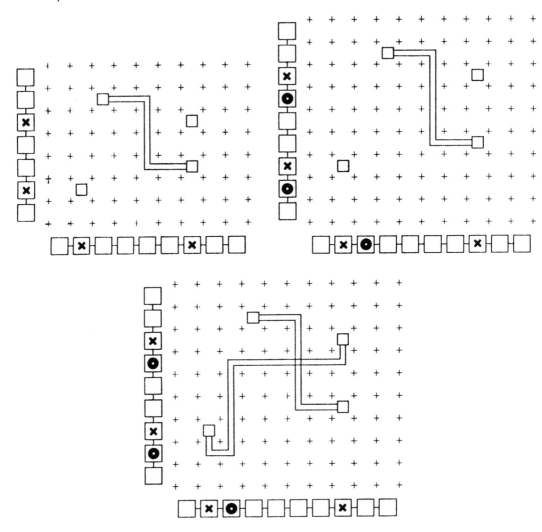

Figure 6-8: Routing an edge by slicing.

There are two important operations that must be performed during the layout
algorithm—slicing a layout to route an edge and combining two sublayouts into a
single layout.   Routing a new edge between two vertices by slicing can be
accomplished easily by the following procedure, which is illustrated in Figure 6-8.

1. For each of the vertices, FIND the x-set and the y-set to which it belongs.

2. Adjacent to these x- and y-sets in the linked lists, insert new x- and y-sets, effectively adding new slices of layout. Because pointers represent the horizontal and vertical components of previously routed edges, the components are not severed and reconnected as was described in Section 5.2. Instead, they "stretch" automatically.

3. Add the new points for the edge to be routed to the appropriate x- and y-sets, and route the edge using pointers to represent the edge components. Each new point belongs to the x- and y-sets of the previous two steps.

Because we are considering only those classes of graphs that have bounded vertex degree, the number of edges to be routed during the entire course of execution of the layout procedure is linear in n, the number of vertices in the input graph. The routing algorithm above is called once for each edge, and hence the total number of invocations is linear in n. During each invocation, a constant number of FIND's are executed, and the rest of the work takes only constant time. Thus the overall cost is the time to execute a linear number of FIND's plus another term which is linear. Since each FIND requires more than constant time, the linear number of FIND's dominates.

The cost of the FIND's cannot be determined without also knowing the number of UNION's that must be performed. The layout algorithm uses the UNION operation in the following procedure, which combines two layouts into one. (Without loss of generality, assume the layouts are side-by-side in x.)

1. Append one linked list of x-sets to the other. This will produce a list of x-sets for the combined layout such that all of the x-coordinates of one sublayout lie to one side of all the x-coordinates of the other.

2. Traverse both linked lists of y-sets, and UNION corresponding y-sets to produce the linked list of y-sets for the the resultant layout. That is, the kth y-set of the final layout is obtained from the UNION of the kth y-sets of the sublayouts.

The time to merge two layouts is dominated by the time to do the UNION's.

The number of UNION's varies each time two layouts are combined because it is dependent upon the lengths of the linked lists that are merged. If σ_R is the aspect ratio of R, the rectangle that contains the combined layout, then the length of the linked list is $\sqrt{\sigma_R A_S(n)}$ since R is always bisected parallel to its short side. This leads to the following recurrence which describes the total number of UNION's executed by the layout algorithm: $U(n) = 0$ for $n = 1$, and

$$U(n) \;=\; U(\alpha n) + U((1-\alpha)n) + \sqrt{\sigma_R A_S(n)}$$

for $n > 1$, where α varies in the range $\alpha_S \leq \alpha \leq 1-\alpha_S$ and σ_R varies in the range $\sigma_S \leq \sigma_R \leq 1-\sigma_S$. This recurrence equation is similar to Recurrence (6–5) which describes time devoted to the execution of the separator subroutine. In fact, the same asymptotic results enumerated in Table 6–6 are valid when $\sqrt{A_S(n)}$ is substituted for $s(n)$. Notice in particular that if $A_S(n) = O(n^q)$ for some $q < 2$, then $U(n) = \Theta(n)$.

We now have a relationship between the area of the layout $A_S(n)$ and the number of UNION's $U(n)$. But $A_S(n)$ was determined, after all, by $f(n)$, the width of the separator. (Do not confuse $f(n)$ with $s(n)$, the time required to execute the separator subroutine.) Carrying this relationship through, the number of UNION's $U(n)$ can be expressed in terms of $f(n)$, and then, using the fact that there are only a linear number of FIND's, the total time required by the management of the layout representation can be determined. Table 6–9 enumerates these results, where $T(n)$ is the time required by the bookkeeping to lay out a graph of n vertices.

The first line of the table can be derived by observing that if $f(n) = O(n^q)$ for $q < 1$ and is monotonic if $f(n) = \Omega(\sqrt{n})$, then $A_S(n) = \Omega(n^{2q})$ and, as was noticed earlier, $U(n) = \Theta(n)$. Because the total number of FIND's is also linear in n, the total time required for bookkeeping is $O(na(n, n))$.

The second line of the table gives the worst-case running time for the bookkeeping that occurs when there is no better than an n-separator theorem. In

Table 6-9: Time devoted to the management of the layout representation.

$f(n)$	$T(n)$
$O(n^q),\ q < 1$†	$\Theta(na(n, n))$
$\Theta(n)$	$\Theta(n \lg n)$

†The function $f(n)$ must also be monotonic if $f(n) = \Omega(n^{1/2})$.

this case the area given by the layout procedure is $\Theta(n^2)$, and the time to combine layouts is $O(n \lg n)$. Other bounds are readily derived for cases when the growth of $f(n)$ lies between n^q for $q < 1$ and n. For example, if $f(n) = n/\lg n$, then the time for bookkeeping is $O(n \lg\lg n)$. Thus even if the separator algorithm is only marginally good, the bookkeeping time is nearly linear.

CHAPTER 7

Further Layout Results

7.1 Introduction

The results of the previous chapter can be applied to other layout problems. Section 7.2 considers layouts where vertices are required to lie on a straight line. The results for this model can be easily generalized to the model where all vertices are constrained to lie on the (convex) perimeter of the layout. The techniques of Chapter 6 are employed to provide area bounds for graphs based on separator theorems for the graphs. In addition some lower bounds are presented that demonstrate the optimality of the constructions for trees and planar graphs.

Section 7.3 contains a design for an $O(n\lg^2 n)$ area chip that can be configured to implement any tree of processors by making only n solder-dot connections such as are used in gate-arrays. If n connections can be broken as well, there is an $O(n\lg n)$ area design which can be configured to implement any tree. These results can be generalized to arbitrary graphs.

Section 7.4 considers how a complete binary tree may be partitioned into chips. The major constraint in chip partitioning is the limit on the number of off-chip connections or *pins*. An arbitrarily large, complete binary tree can be built from a single type of chip whose pin count is independent of the size of the tree and whose chip area is efficiently utilized.

7.2 Layouts with Collinear Vertices[17]

Figure 7-1 shows how an $f(n)$-separator theorem can be used to construct a layout with collinear vertices. First, the graph is bisected by cutting at most $c_S f(n)$ edges. Then layouts are recursively constructed for the subgraphs and are placed side-by-side along the *baseline*. Vertical slices are made through the layouts, and edges are routed in the space above.

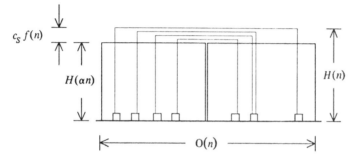

Figure 7-1: The construction of a layout with collinear vertices.

The analysis of this construction is much easier than that in Section 6.3. Since at most two vertical slices are made for each edge, the length of the layout along the baseline is $O(n)$. The height $H(n)$ of the layout is a constant for $n = 1$, and

$$H(n) \;=\; \max_{\alpha_S \le \alpha \le 1 - \alpha_S} H(\alpha n) + c_S f(n)$$

for $n > 1$.

If $f(n)$ is nondecreasing, then $H(n) = O(f(n)\lg n)$ and the total area $A_S(n)$ is therefore $O(f(n) n \lg n)$. In particular, if $f(n) = O(\lg^k n)$, then $A_S(n) = O(n\lg^{k+1} n)$. If $f(n)$ is $\Omega(n^q)$ for some $q > 0$ and $f(n)$ satisfies Regularity Condition C1, then $H(n) = O(f(n))$ and $A_S(n) = O(nf(n))$.

This means that planar graphs can be embedded on a line in $O(n\sqrt{n})$ area and

---

[17]Of the research reported in this section, the the upper bounds on the areas of trees and planar graphs represent joint work with my advisor, Jon L. Bentley.

trees in $O(n \lg n)$ area. We now show that these embeddings for trees and planar graphs are optimal to within a constant factor. A similar result on trees was independently discovered by Brent and Kung [7], who show that in any layout of a complete binary tree, the area devoted to wire must have order at least $n \lg n$. The approach here differs in that we show that the convex region containing the layout must have $\Omega(n \lg n)$ area.

> **Lemma 7-1:** For any complete-binary-tree layout of $n = 2^k - 1$ collinear vertices where $k \geq 0$, there exists a perpendicular to the baseline that lies between the leftmost and rightmost vertices and cuts at least $\lceil k/2 \rceil$ edges and vertices.

Proof. (Induction.) The lemma is easily satisfied for the initial cases of $n = 1$ and $n = 3$. For the general case, consider the four subtrees of size $2^{k-2} - 1$. (See Figure 7-2.) Call the leaf that is leftmost on the baseline v, and let w be the rightmost leaf that is in a different subtree from v. Choose one of the two subtrees that contain neither v nor w. The inductive hypothesis gives us a perpendicular that cuts $\lceil (k-2)/2 \rceil$ edges or vertices in the subtree. Since v and w are in different halfplanes as determined by the perpendicular, the path between them must be cut by the perpendicular. But this path is disjoint from the subtree, which means that one more edge or vertex is cut for a total of $\lceil k/2 \rceil$. $\square$

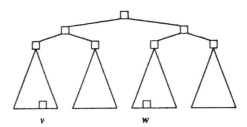

Figure 7-2: The construction in Lemma 7-1.

This lemma can be used to show that the minimum area of any convex region containing a layout for a complete binary tree must be $\Omega(n \lg n)$. The length of the layout along the baseline must be $\Omega(n)$, and as demonstrated by the previous construction, there is a point in the layout $\Omega(\lg n)$ away from the baseline. This point and the two points on the limits of the baseline determine a triangle which has $\Omega(n \lg n)$ area. Since any convex region that contains these three points must contain the triangle, so must any convex region containing the layout have $\Omega(n \lg n)$ area.

Similarly, the $O(n\sqrt{n})$ upper bound on the area for the layout of an n-vertex planar graph is tight to within a constant factor because a square mesh requires $\Omega(n\sqrt{n})$ area. This can be shown by considering that the minimum bisection width of an n-vertex square mesh is $\sqrt{n}$. Thus the perpendicular to the baseline that divides the vertices on the baseline into $\lfloor n/2 \rfloor$ and $\lceil n/2 \rceil$ vertices must cut $\sqrt{n}$ edges. The rest of the proof follows that for the complete binary tree.

The lower bound results here generalize immediately to the model in which all vertices are constrained to lie on the perimeter of a convex region. The perimeter of the region must have length $\Omega(n)$ since there are n vertices on it. The diameter of the region (the line segment that realizes the greatest distance between two points) must also be $\Omega(n)$ since it is no less than a factor of π times the length of the perimeter. Applying the techniques of the previous construction and using the diameter of the region as a baseline yields the same lower bound results as before. In the case of the mesh, an exact bisection by a perpendicular may not be possible because some vertices may lie on the perpendicular itself. This situation can be avoided (see [41]) by putting a unit jog in the perpendicular so that it looks like a lowercase aitch without a left leg. The "perpendicular" can then be adjusted vertically to bisect the graph.

For the standard VLSI model in which vertices need not be collinear, a similar construction shows that minimum dimension of any layout of a complete binary tree must be $\Omega(\lg n)$.

7.3 Configurable Layouts

One of the attractions of the ROM, PLA, or gate-array approaches to integrated circuit designs is that one layout organization can be customized for a particular application without disrupting the overall geometry of the layout. For example, the bits of a ROM memory can be set without affecting its layout. The choice of minterms for a PLA can change while the layout for the PLA remains about the same. In the gate-array approach, one chip is produced with unconnected wires running in channels between the components. The chip is configured by adding *solder dots* to connect the wires, but the overall structure remains the same. This philosophy of design can be applied to graph layouts.

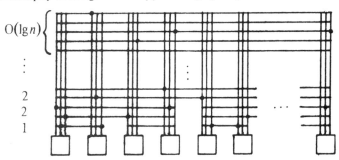

Figure 7-3: A layout that can configure any tree.

Figure 7-3 shows an $O(n \lg^2 n)$ area layout for a chip which can implement any binary tree of n vertices by simply adding n solder dots. The organization of this chip is based on the collinear layouts of Section 7.2. All of the vertices are lined up on the baseline and their connections run vertically. Parallel to the baseline are $\lg^2 n$ horizontal wires. The top $O(\lg n)$ wires run all the way across the layout. The next $O(\lg n)$ are broken halfway. The third group are broken into four, and so forth. Placing solder dots on the intersections of the horizontal and vertical wires connects the vertices.

To decide where to put the solder dots, we use the fact that any binary tree with n vertices can be bisected into $\lfloor n/2 \rfloor$ and $\lceil n/2 \rceil$ vertices by cutting $O(\lg n)$

edges. This exact bisection result follows immediately from the one-separator theorem for trees. Observe that the layout without its top $O(\lg n)$ wires forms two smaller versions of itself. Thus the two sets of vertices can be recursively laid out on either side of the halfway break. Then the two sublayouts are combined. Each edge in the cut set is mapped to one of the top $O(\lg n)$ horizontal wires. Two solder dots are placed on each horizontal wire to connect the two vertices incident on the corresponding edge.

If the horizontal wires are considered to be buses, several solder dots can connect the output of one processor to the inputs of many others. Using this interpretation, the layout can be configured to implement any tree no matter what its vertex degrees. A vertex-separator theorem such as that of [25] is used in this instance to determine where the solder dots go.

The approach will work for more than just trees, of course. If the class of graphs has an $f(n)$-separator theorem where $f(n) = \Omega(n^q)$ for some $q > 0$, then a layout whose area is $O(n\,f(n))$ can be configured to implement any graph of n vertices in the class. If $f(n) = \Theta(n)$, the design degenerates to a crosspoint switch.

Sometimes it is just as easy to break as make connections. When this alternative is available, any tree can be configured from an $O(n \lg n)$ area layout. The collinear layout results of the previous section lead directly to such a design. Wires placed in the horizontal channels are broken along a horizontal line when the vertices are partitioned by the separator theorem. For classes of graphs with an $f(n)$-separator theorem where $f(n) = \Omega(n^q)$ for $q > 0$, the ability to break connections gives at most a constant factor improvement in area over the previous design when this technique is used.

7.4 Packaging a Complete Binary Tree

Although integrated circuit technology is advancing at a breathtaking pace, one sector of that technology is crawling in comparison. The number of external connections from an integrated circuit chip is severely limited. Whereas some enthusiastic technologists project an eye-opening 10^8 components per chip, two hundred pins per chip seems a large number to most. A chip that requires many more is unlikely to be realizable for quite some time.

A complete binary tree is an attractive structure from this point of view if the tree fits entirely on one chip and the root is the only off-chip connection. Several researchers [3, 8, 23, 36] have proposed, however, that much larger tree systems be built. (See also Section 3.2.) When any system is larger than a single chip, it becomes necessary to partition it among separate chips that can be assembled at the printed circuit level. What is the most effective way to partition a large complete binary tree among chips?

Figure 7–4 shows the partitioning proposed in [23]. Each of the squares in the diagram represents a chip packed as full as possible with an H-tree layout (Figure 5–2, page 83). The rectangle above is another chip which contains the standard $O(n \lg n)$ layout (Figure 5–1, page 82), but with leaves connected off chip. This second chip can be used repeatedly to combine several smaller complete binary trees into a larger. Thus with two kinds of chips, a complete binary tree of any size can be built up. At the printed circuit level, the structure is a complete k-ary tree where $k+1$ is the number of off-chip data paths.

We can do better. Figure 7–5 shows how arbitrarily large complete binary trees can be built out of a single chip that has only four off-chip connections. Each chip contains one internal node of the tree, and the remainder of the chip is packed as full as possible with an H-tree layout. The internal node requires three off-chip connections (denoted F, R, and L in the figure) for its father, right son, and left son. The H-tree requires only one off-chip connection (denoted T) to its father.

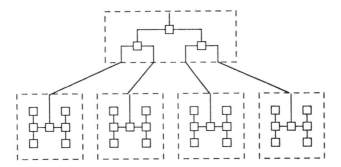

Figure 7-4: An inefficient partitioning of a complete binary tree into chips.

To interconnect two chips, the unconnected internal node on one of the two chips is selected as the father of the two H-trees. (In Figure 7-5 the internal node on the left has been chosen for this purpose.) The R pin on this chip is connected to its own T pin, and the L pin is connected to the T pin on the other chip. Considered as a unit, the combined two chips now have the same structure as a single chip— three connections to an internal node and one to the root of a complete binary tree. The pair of chips can be similarly combined with another pair to produce a quadruple of chips, which can in turn be combined, and so forth. Figure 7-6 shows a large complete binary tree which has been wired up in this recursive fashion.

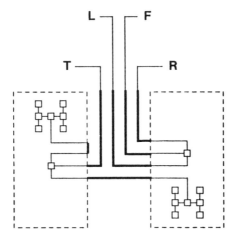

Figure 7-5: Only one kind of chip is needed to package a complete binary tree.

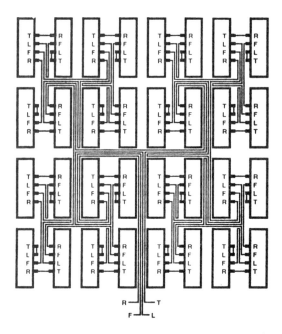

Figure 7-6: A large complete binary tree built up from a single kind of chip.

The one-chip method has many advantages over the two-chip method. Most obviously, the one-chip method uses only one kind of chip. Why manufacture two kinds when one will do? Second, there are only four data paths that go off chip. The only way the two-chip solution can match this is if the chip with the standard layout has exactly one internal node on it. Third, the chip used in the one-chip method is packed full. The other method leaves the chip with the standard layout almost empty. Since the cost of an implementation is almost directly related to the number of chips required [5], the same size tree can be built for less with the one-chip solution. Finally, the layout of the printed circuit board is linear in the number of chips using the one-chip method. The two-chip solution gives an $O(n \lg n)$ printed circuit layout. Although the case is not particularly strong for asymptotic analysis of printed circuit layout, the constant factors give a clear preference to the more regular, linear area layout. If circumstances permit, the wires connecting the chips can in fact be routed underneath the chips themselves, thereby requiring no more area on the printed circuit board than the chips themselves.

Conclusion

Systolic Systems

Systolic structures provide a model of parallel VLSI computation that takes into account issues such as I/0, control, and interprocessor communication. In a systolic system pipelining and multiprocessing occur simultaneously to ensure high throughput and fast response. The systolic approach is not the answer to every VLSI problem, but when it does apply, good algorithms that work well in practice are a consequence. (For a practical demonstration of this design philosophy, see [12].)

Since communication in a systolic system is through fixed interconnections, it is desirable in a VLSI implementation that these data paths have simple and regular geometries. This thesis has concentrated primarily on systolic algorithms for arrays and trees out of this concern. Part II showed that these are not the only graphs with good layouts, however.

Among the contributions of Part I is a design methodology for systolic systems. An algorithm can be designed in the more flexible design space of semisystolic systems and transformed by the Systolic Conversion Lemma (Lemma 2-1) into a systolic system. The most important corollary of this lemma is the Broadcast Corollary (Corollary 2-4), which shows that for any systolic system augmented by broadcasting, there is an equivalent systolic system with no broadcasting. The Broadcast Corollary allows a designer to build systems that behave as if the processors operate on global data, but without global communication.

The Reset Theorem (Theorem 2-6) provides a transformation that maps algorithms from the design space of semisystolic systems back into the design space. This transformation is orthogonal to the Systolic Conversion Lemma in the sense that if the Systolic Conversion Lemma could be applied to an algorithm before the transformation, it can be applied after. The view from the host is that a global action has taken place in a single pulsation, yet the work is in fact distributed across time using local connections.

The other general result, Lemma 2-5, parallels earlier work by Cole [9] and Smith [35] in the realm of cellular automata. We have extended this result to all semisystolic systems. In addition, the ideas of real-time computation pioneered by these two researchers have been extended by this thesis.

The general results of Chapter 2 gave way to many particular algorithms in Chapter 3. Many interesting varieties of real-time priority queues were developed including the systolic multiqueue and one which operates on variable-length keys. The results were extended to the real-time maintenance of order statistics and a pipelined search tree. In addition, a real-time, binary up-down counter and a real-time pattern matcher were designed. The descriptions of these algorithms would have been substantially more complicated without the Systolic Conversion Lemma.

Chapter 4 showed how systolic arrays can efficiently perform matrix computations. Matrix-vector multiplication, solving of triangular linear systems, convolution, discrete Fourier transform, and filtering can all be computed on linearly connected systolic arrays. Matrix multiplication and LU-decomposition can both be performed on hex-connected systolic arrays.

For the important problem of solving a dense system of n linear equations in $O(n)$ time on n^2 mesh-connected processors, the LU-decomposition algorithm improves upon the matrix inversion algorithm of Van Scoy [43]. LU-decomposition is to be preferred to matrix inversion [10] particularly for band matrices which typically have dense inverses. Furthermore, the hardware requirements for the

LU-decomposition algorithm are only a function of the band's width, not its length. Finally, the all-important problem of host-device communication has been addressed, where the band-matrix solution has the advantage of pipelining.

Systolic systems treat the costs due to interprocessor communication explicitly. These costs will likely be a dominant factor in the overall cost of computation in VLSI systems as they are for other parallel systems. Systolic systems can help bridge the gap between theory and practice because these costs are modeled explicitly. When a systolic system is built as an actual VLSI chip, its behavior obeys the mathematics of a computational theory.

Layouts

The layout algorithm of Part II should be viewed in an historical context. Most wire-routing programs for printed circuit boards have two phases. First, the chips are placed on the printed circuit board. Then leaving the chips fixed, wires are routed one by one using heuristic search—usually a variant on the path-finding algorithm attributed to Lee [22]. Most hardware designers concede that the first of these two steps is the harder. With a good placement, routing is easy; with a bad placement, routing is impossible.

Most routers for integrated circuits use much the same approach. Variations include *polycells* [26] and *gate arrays*. In the polycell approach the components are laid down in horizontal strips and the channels between the strips are used for routing the wires. The advantage is that the channel width is not fixed. If a channel has too much congestion, extra tracks can be added easily in a manner reminiscent of slicing. The channels run both horizontally and vertically in gate arrays, but are a fixed width determined in advance. Typically, all cells are identical and are connected up with a final layer of metalization.

Recently, Johannsen [18] has introduced *bristle blocks* as a technique for laying out integrated circuits. Rather than using standard wire routing to connect cells in a design, the cells plug together. This would seem to mean that all cells must have the same width or *pitch*. Instead, however, the cells are designed with places to stretch so that a cell with smaller pitch can be adjusted to plug into a wider cell with no routing necessary.

The idea of using divide-and-conquer to help with the general wire-routing problem is not new. As far back as 1969, Günther [15] gave a heuristic procedure for arranging machines in a workshop given the frequency of travel between machines. This algorithm, which applies as much to circuit placement as to machine placement, partitions the transportation graph and places the subgraphs in subrectangles of the original area. Günther's technique for partitioning is highly heuristic, and he comments that it is the critical step. Another heuristic for graph partitioning is given by Kernighan and Lin [19]. Among the applications they mention is that of partitioning chips among printed circuit boards so as to minimize the connections between boards. There is an algorithmic solution to the partitioning problem, however. It is based on the fact that the graphs of interconnections that arise in practice are almost planar. By replacing each crossover in some drawing of the graph with an artificial vertex that performs the crossover, Lipton and Tarjan's separator algorithm for planar graphs can be applied.

It is unlikely that a fast general partitioning algorithm will be found because the problem of finding the minimum bisection width of a graph is NP-complete [13]. In other words, graphs are hard to partition. This unfortunate situation brings up the question, *"Can the divide-and-conquer approach used in this paper, which performs placement and routing simultaneously, compete with or enhance those techniques already in use?"*

A difficulty with applying the techniques of this paper concerns constant factors in the areas of layouts. The model in Section 5.2 assumes that each vertex fits into a square of the grid, and furthermore, that the sizes of vertices and edges are comparable. For many practical applications, the vertices are somewhat larger than the edges. This means that the grid size is substantially larger than the edge width, and thus each slice through the layout wastes a large constant factor. A solution to this problem is to design the cells represented by vertices with places where they can be sliced, and then use the largest unsliceable portion of a cell as the granularity of the grid. This technique complements the bristle blocks approach because places where a cell can stretch are frequently places where it can be sliced.

There is another solution, however, which does not require the cells to be sliceable, and yet does allow the granularity of the grid to be the width of a wire. The limitation is that sizes and shapes of vertices must not vary widely. Each vertex is placed in a rectangle whose area is four times the area of the vertex. The layout algorithm is allowed to slice this rectangle, but slicing is allowed only in one direction. In the other direction the space between or next to the layouts is used as a channel for routing. When a slice is made through a vertex, the vertex is not sliced, but instead the edge simply crosses over on another layer. When the algorithm terminates, each edge that crosses over a vertex is routed around the vertex in the unused area provided by the rectangle.

Where vertices are large, unsliceable, and of widely varying sizes, the problem becomes one of two-dimensional bin-packing with constraints. This formulation seems the least tractable. It may be, however, that as with bin-packing, simple heuristics can be found that give reasonable solutions for commonly occuring instances.

In summary, this thesis has shown that a good separator theorem for a class of graphs is a sufficient condition for there to be a good VLSI layout of any graph in the class. This led to linear area layouts for trees which have a one-separator theorem and $O(n \lg^2 n)$ area layouts for planar graphs which have a $\sqrt{n}$-separator theorem. A general algorithm was presented that lays out these particular graphs in $O(n \lg n)$ time. Most of the computation goes to executing the separator algorithm for the graphs—the time devoted to management of the layout representation is nearly linear.

The divide-and-conquer techniques apply to other models including that in which all vertices are constrained to be collinear. The layout results of this model were applied to a study of configurable layouts. It was shown, for example, that $O(n \lg^2 n)$ area is sufficient to implement a reconfigurable layout that can implement any tree by only adding n solder-dot connections. If n connections can be broken as well, there is an $O(n \lg n)$ area layout.

Among the peripheral results of Part II was the fact that any VLSI layout, no matter how long and skinny, can be reembedded in a square whose area is at most three times the area of the original layout. Also, a design was proposed for the partitioning of a complete binary tree into identical chips.

Acknowledgments

Few theses are written in a vacuum, and I am pleased to have written mine in the warm environment of the Carnegie-Mellon University Computer Science Department. The cohesiveness of that community allowed the cross-fertilization of ideas from different disciplines within computer science and provided me with the exciting opportunity to explore integrated circuits from a theoretical perspective.

No student could have had more attention and encouragement from two premier computer scientists than I had from my advisors Jon L. Bentley and H. T. Kung. From Jon I learned about algorithm design and the importance of seeking simple formulations of ideas. Kung taught me the central issues of parallel computation and offered me wise and enlightened advice about my academic career.

I spent many hours with Jim Saxe sorting through the details of my thesis. Jim taught me about recurrences (the hard kind) and provided me with constant feedback about my ideas.

Bob Sproull and Leo Guibas were good enough to serve on my thesis committee. Both provided me with excellent comments concerning the organization and substance of my thesis.

I profited from many discussions with Mike Foster, Peter Schwarz, and Clark Thompson. Rick Gumpertz deserves special thanks for finding and removing the bugs I identified in Scribe while producing the thesis. Inna Sverbilov helped prepare the index and figures for the MIT Press version. I would also like to thank David Reed and Andrew Palay for the dover hacking that allowed me to print my thesis at MIT.

127

I am especially grateful to the Fannie and John Hertz Foundation which provided me with a fellowship during my graduate education.

My wife and lover Linda Lue deserves more than thanks. She kept me sane during the most difficult moments of thesis writing, and she devoted her energy to our marriage and family so that I could pursue my degree. My love for computer science shrivels in comparison with my love for her. This thesis is as much hers as it is mine.

References

1. Alfred V. Aho, John E. Hopcroft, and Jeffrey D. Ullman, *The Design and Analysis of Computer Algorithms,* Addison-Wesley, Reading, Massachusetts, 1974.

2. Michael O. Albertson and Joan P. Hutchinson, "On the independence ratio of a graph," *Journal of Graph Theory,* Vol. 2, 1978, pp. 1–8.

3. Jon Louis Bentley and H. T. Kung, "A tree machine for searching problems," *Proceedings of the 1979 International Conference on Parallel Processing,* IEEE, 1979, pp. 257–266.

4. Jon Louis Bentley, Dorthea Haken, and James B. Saxe, "A general method for solving divide-and-conquer recurrences," Technical report CMU–CS–78–154, Department of Computer Science, Carnegie-Mellon University, December 1978.

5. Thomas R. Blakeslee, *Digital Design with Standard MSI and LSI,* John Wiley & Sons, New York, 1975.

6. R. P. Brent and H. T. Kung, "Fast algorithms for manipulating formal power series," *Journal of the Association for Computing Machinery,* Vol. 25, October 1978, pp. 581–595.

7. R. P. Brent and H. T. Kung, "On the area of binary tree layouts," Technical report TR–CS–79–07, The Australian National University, Department of Computer Science, July 1979.

8. Sally A. Browning, *The Tree Machine: A Highly Concurrent Computing Environment,* Ph.D. dissertation, Computer Science Department, California Institute of Technology, January 1980.

9. Stephen N. Cole, "Real-time computation by n-dimensional iterative arrays of finite-state machines," *IEEE Transactions on Computers,* Vol. C–18, April 1969, pp. 349–365.

10. G. Dahlquist, A. Björck, and N. Anderson, *Numerical Methods,* Prentice-Hall, Englewood Cliffs, New Jersey, 1969.

11. Robert W. Floyd and Jeffrey D. Ullman, "The compilation of regular expressions into integrated circuits," *21st Annual Symposium on Foundations of Computer Science,* IEEE Computer Society, October 1980.

12. Michael J. Foster and H. T. Kung, "The design of special-purpose VLSI chips," *Computer Magazine,* Vol. 13, No. 13, January 1980, pp. 26–40, An early version of this paper entitled "Design of special-purpose VLSI chips: examples and opinions" appears in *Proceedings of the 7th International Symposium on Computer Architecture,* La Baule, France, May 1980.

13. M. R. Garey, D. S. Johnson, and L. Stockmeyer, "Some simplified polynomial complete problems," *6th Annual Symposium on Theory of Computing,* ACM, April 1974, pp. 47–63.

14. Leonidas J. Guibas, Private communication, March 1980 .

15. Th. Günther, "Die räumliche anordnung von einheiten mit wechselbeziehungen," *Elektronische Datenverarbeitung,* May 1969, pp. 209–212.

16. Frederick C. Hennie III, *Iterative Arrays of Logical Circuits,* M. I. T. Press and John Wiley Sons, Inc., M. I. T. Press Research Monographs, 1961.

17. Dan Hoey and Charles E. Leiserson, "A layout for the shuffle-exchange network," *1980 International Conference on Parallel Processing,* August 1980, pp. 329–336.

18. Dave Johannsen, "Bristle blocks: a silicon compiler," *Proceedings of the Caltech Conference on Very Large Scale Integration,* Pasadena, California, January 1979, pp. 303–310.

19. B. W. Kernighan and S. Lin, "An effective heuristic procedure for partitioning graphs," *Bell Systems Technical Journal,* Vol. 49, February 1970, pp. 291–308.

20. H. T. Kung, "Let's design algorithms for VLSI systems," *Proceedings of the Caltech Conference on Very Large Scale Integration,* Charles L. Seitz, ed., Pasadena, California, January 1979, pp. 65–90.

21. H. T. Kung and Charles E. Leiserson, "Systolic arrays (for VLSI)," *Sparse Matrix Proceedings 1978,* I. S. Duff and G. W. Stewart, ed., Society for Industrial and Applied Mathematics, 1979, pp. 256–282, An early version appears in Section 8.3 of [28].

22. C. Y. Lee, "An algorithm for path connection and its applications," *IRE Transactions on Electronic Computers,* Vol. EC–10, No. 3, September 1961, pp. 346–365.

23. Charles E. Leiserson, "Systolic priority queues," *Proceedings of the Caltech Conference on Very Large Scale Integration*, Charles L. Seitz, ed., California Institute of Technology, Pasadena, California, January 1979, pp. 199–214.

24. P. M. Lewis, R. E. Stearns, and J. Hartmanis, "Memory bounds for recognition of context-free and context-sensitive languages," *IEEE Symposium on Switching Circuit Theory and Logical Design*, IEEE, 1965.

25. Richard J. Lipton and Robert E. Tarjan, "A separator theorem for planar graphs," *A Conference on Theoretical Computer Science*, University of Waterloo, August 1977.

26. Roland L. Mattison, "A high quality, low cost router for MOS/LSI," *Proceedings of the ACM-IEEE Design Automation Workshop*, Dallas, Texas, June 1972, pp. 94–103.

27. R. McNaughton and H. Yamada, "Regular expressions and state graphs for automata," *IEEE Transactions on Computers*, Vol. 9, No. 1, March 1960, pp. 39–47.

28. Carver A. Mead and Lynn A. Conway, *Introduction to VLSI Systems*, Addison-Wesley, Reading, Massachusetts, 1980.

29. Carver Mead and Martin Rem, "Cost and performance of VLSI computing structures," *IEEE Journal of Solid State Circuits*, Vol. SC–14, No. 2, April 1979, pp. 455–462.

30. George H. Mealy, "A method for synthesizing sequential circuits," *Bell Systems Technical Journal*, Vol. 34, No. 5, September 1955, pp. 1045–1079.

31. Edward F. Moore, "Gedanken-experiments on sequential machines," In *Automata Studies*, Princeton University Press, Princeton, New Jersey, Annals of Mathematics StudiesNo. 34, 1956, pp. 129–153.

32. Yu. Orfman, "On the algorithmic complexity of discrete functions," English translation in *Soviet Physics—Doklady*, Vol. 7, No. 7, 1963, pp. 589–591.

33. Franco P. Preparata and Jean Vuillemin, "The cube-connected-cycles: a versatile network for parallel computation," Technical report 356, Institut de Recherche d'Informatique et d'Automatique, June 1979.

34. C. H. Séquin, A. M. Despain, and D. A. Patterson, "Communication in X-tree, a modular multiprocessor system," *ACM 78 Proceedings*, ACM, 1978.

35. Alvy Ray Smith III, "Cellular automata theory," Technical report SEL–70–016, Stanford Electronics Laboratory, December 1969.

36. S. W. Song, "A highly concurrent tree machine for database applications," *1980 International Conference on Parallel Processing*, August 1980, pp. 259–268.

37. Harold S. Stone, "Parallel processing with the perfect shuffle," *IEEE Transactions on Computers*, Vol. C–20, No. 2, February 1971, pp. 153–161.

38. I. E. Sutherland and C. A. Mead, "Microelectronics and computer science," *Scientific American*, Vol. 237, No. 3, September 1977, pp. 210–228.

39. Ivan E. Sutherland and Donald Oestreicher, "How big should a printed circuit board be?" *IEEE Transactions on Computers*, Vol. C–22, May 1973, pp. 537–542.

40. Robert Endre Tarjan, "Efficiency of a good but not linear set union algorithm," *Journal of the Association for Computing Machinery*, Vol. 25, No. 2, 1975, pp. 215–225.

41. Clark D. Thompson, *A Complexity Theory for VLSI*, Ph.D. dissertation, Department of Computer Science, Carnegie-Mellon University, 1980.

42. L. G. Valiant, "Universality considerations in VLSI circuits," December 1979, draft (to appear in *IEEE Transactions on Computers*).

43. Frances Lucretia Van Scoy, *Parallel Algorithms in Cellular Spaces*, Ph.D. dissertation, School of Engineering and Applied Sciences, University of Virginia, May 1976.

Index